First World War
and Army of Occupation
War Diary
France, Belgium and Germany

25 DIVISION
7 Infantry Brigade
Loyal North Lancashire Regiment
8th Battalion
24 September 1915 - 10 February 1918

WO95/2243/2

The Naval & Military Press Ltd
www.nmarchive.com
Published in association with The National Archives

Published by

The Naval & Military Press Ltd

Unit 10 Ridgewood Industrial Park,

Uckfield, East Sussex,

TN22 5QE England

Tel: +44 (0) 1825 749494

www.naval-military-press.com

www.nmarchive.com

This diary has been reprinted in facsimile from the original. Any imperfections are inevitably reproduced and the quality may fall short of modern type and cartographic standards.

© Crown Copyright
Images reproduced by permission of The National Archives, London, England, 2015.

Contents

Document type	Place/Title	Date From	Date To
Heading	WO95/2243/2		
Heading	8th Bn Loyal Nth Lancs Sep 1915-Feb 1918 Disbanded Feb 1918		
Heading	8th Bn Loyal Nth Lancs Sep-Oct 1915		
Heading	War Diary Of 8th Battn Loyal N Lanc Rgt From Sept 24-Oct 31 1915 (Volume I)		
War Diary		24/09/1915	31/10/1915
Heading	25th Division 8th L. N. Lancs Vol 2 Nov 15 To Feb 18		
Heading	War Diary Of 8th (Ser) Battn Loyal North Lanc Regt from Nov 1-30 1915 Volume 2		
War Diary		01/11/1915	30/11/1915
Heading	25th Div 8th L. N. Lancs Vol 3 December 1915		
Heading	War Diary Of 8th (S) Battalion Loyal N. Lanc. Rgt. From Dec 1-31 Volume 3		
War Diary		01/12/1915	31/12/1915
Miscellaneous	Routine Orders By Brigadier General Cmdg 7th Infantry Brigade.	12/12/1915	12/12/1915
Operation(al) Order(s)	7th Infantry Brigade Order No. 6	23/12/1915	23/12/1915
Heading	8th Battalion Loyal North Lancashire Regiment January 1916		
Heading			
Heading	War Diary of 8th (Nov) Battn Loyal North Lancashire Regt From 1st January 1916 To 31st January 1916 (Volume No 4)		
War Diary		01/01/1916	31/01/1916
Miscellaneous			
Heading	8th Battalion Loyal North Lancashire Regiment February 1916		
Miscellaneous			
Heading	War Diary 8th Battn Loyal North Lanc Regt From Feb 1-29 1916 Volume 5		
War Diary	Outtersteene	01/02/1916	29/02/1916
Heading	8th Battalion Loyal North Lancashire Regiment. March 1916		
Miscellaneous			
Heading	War Diary Of 8th Bn Loyal North Lancashire Regt From 1st March To 31st March 1916 (Volume No 6)		
Miscellaneous			
War Diary	Outtersteene	01/03/1916	10/03/1916
War Diary	La Pierriere	10/03/1916	11/03/1916
War Diary	Hestrus	11/03/1916	14/03/1916
War Diary	Maizieres	15/03/1916	31/03/1916
Heading	8th Battalion Loyal North Lancashire Regiment April 1916		
Miscellaneous			
Heading	War Diary Of 8th Bn Loyal North Lancashire Regt From 1st April 1916 To 30th April 1916 (Volume 7)		
War Diary	Maizieres	01/04/1916	11/04/1916
War Diary	Maroeuil	12/04/1916	30/04/1916

Heading	8th Battalion Loyal North Lancashire Regiment May 1916		
Heading			
Heading	War Diary Of 8th Bn Loyal North Lancashire Regt. From 1st May 1916 To 31st May 1916 (Volume 8)		
War Diary		01/05/1916	31/05/1916
Heading	8th Battalion Loyal North Lancashire Regiment June 1916		
Miscellaneous			
Miscellaneous	LNL-W-1	05/07/1916	05/07/1916
Heading	War Diary Of 8th (Ser) Battn Loyal North Lancashire Regt From 1st June To 30th June 1916		
War Diary	Monchy Breton	01/06/1916	30/06/1916
Heading	8th Battalion Loyal North Lancashires. July 1916		
Miscellaneous			
War Diary	Lealvillers	01/07/1916	29/07/1916
Miscellaneous	Reserve Army Special Order	17/07/1916	17/07/1916
Miscellaneous	Special Order Of The Day By Lieut-General Sir T. L. N. Morland, K. C. B., D.S.O.	17/07/1916	17/07/1916
Miscellaneous	Special Order Of The Day By Brig. General C. E. Heathcote. D.S.O. Commanding 7th Infantry Brigade.		
Miscellaneous	Extract From Routine Orders By Major General E. G. T. Bainbridge C. B. Commanding 25th Division	17/07/1916	17/07/1916
Heading	1/8th Battalion Loyal North Lancashire Regiment August 1916		
Miscellaneous			
War Diary		30/07/1916	31/08/1916
Miscellaneous	Report Of Patrols During Night Of July 31st-August 1st 1916	01/08/1916	01/08/1916
Map			
Heading	8th. Loyal North Lancs. Regt. September 1916		
Miscellaneous			
War Diary	Bouzincourt	01/09/1916	30/09/1916
Heading	8th Battalion Loyal North Lancashire Regiment. October 1916		
Miscellaneous			
War Diary	B.E.F.	01/10/1916	31/10/1916
Heading	8th Battalion Loyal North Lancashire Regiment November 1916		
Miscellaneous			
War Diary	In The Field	01/11/1916	01/12/1916
Heading	8th Battalion Loyal North Lancashire Regiment. December 1916		
Miscellaneous			
War Diary	In The Field	01/12/1916	31/01/1917
Miscellaneous	Awards 423 Battn. Order No. 82		
War Diary	Romarin	01/02/1917	01/02/1917
War Diary	In The Field	02/02/1917	28/02/1917
War Diary	Berthen	01/03/1917	01/03/1917
War Diary	Lynde	11/03/1917	11/03/1917
War Diary	Sec Bois	19/03/1917	20/03/1917
War Diary	Outtersteene	21/03/1917	22/03/1917
War Diary	La Creche	23/03/1917	30/03/1917
War Diary	Kortepyp Camp	31/03/1917	31/03/1917
War Diary	Neuve Eglise	01/04/1917	04/04/1917
War Diary	La Creche	05/04/1917	06/04/1917

Type	Location	From	To
War Diary	Le Bizet	06/04/1917	09/04/1917
War Diary	Front Line	10/04/1917	13/04/1917
War Diary	Le Bizet	14/05/1917	14/05/1917
War Diary	3rd Marie Cappel	15/04/1917	22/04/1917
War Diary	Noote Boom	23/04/1917	30/04/1917
War Diary	Strazeele	01/05/1917	03/05/1917
War Diary	Lynde	04/05/1917	04/05/1917
War Diary	Tatinghem	05/05/1917	17/05/1917
War Diary	Lynde	18/05/1917	18/05/1917
War Diary	Strazeele	19/05/1917	20/05/1917
War Diary	Ravelsberg	20/05/1917	24/05/1917
War Diary	Neuve Eglise	24/05/1917	28/05/1917
War Diary	Trenches Wulverghem Sector	28/05/1917	31/05/1917
War Diary	3rd Worcestershire Regiment.	31/05/1917	31/05/1917
War Diary	Trenches Wulverghem Sector	01/06/1917	11/06/1917
War Diary	Wulverghem	12/06/1917	12/06/1917
War Diary	Neuve Eglise	13/06/1917	13/06/1917
War Diary	Trenches	14/06/1917	22/06/1917
War Diary	Ravelsberg	23/06/1917	27/06/1917
War Diary	Capelle Sur La Lys Area	27/06/1917	30/06/1917
Miscellaneous	To all ranks of 25th Division.	07/06/1917	07/06/1917
War Diary	Capelle Sur La Lys	01/07/1917	30/07/1917
War Diary	Belgian Chateau	31/07/1917	10/08/1917
War Diary	Steenvoorde	11/08/1917	05/09/1917
War Diary	Chateau Segard	06/09/1917	07/09/1917
War Diary	Wippenhoek	08/09/1917	09/09/1917
War Diary	Caestre	10/09/1917	10/09/1917
War Diary	Steenbecque	11/09/1917	11/09/1917
War Diary	Burbure	12/09/1917	03/10/1917
War Diary	Bethune	04/10/1917	31/10/1917
War Diary	Corre	01/11/1917	30/11/1917
War Diary	Reclinghem	01/12/1917	01/12/1917
War Diary	Predefin	02/12/1917	02/12/1917
War Diary	Courcelles-Le-Comte	03/12/1917	04/12/1917
War Diary	Barastre	05/12/1917	22/12/1917
War Diary	Favreuil	22/12/1917	31/01/1918
War Diary		01/02/1918	10/02/1918
Miscellaneous			

W095/22431/2

26TH DIVISION
7TH INFY BDE

8TH BN LOYAL NTH LANCS
SEP 1915 – FEB 1918

Disbanded Feb 1918

25TH DIVISION
(ATTACHED) → 74TH INFY BDE

8TH BN LOYAL NTH LANCS
SEP - OCT 1915
(TO 7TH INFY BDE 31-10-15)

Confidential

War Diary

of

8th Battn. Loyal N. Lancs. Regt.

from Sept 24 — Oct 31
1915 (VOLUME I)

to 7th Div Bn
Oct 1915

Army Form C. 2118.

WAR DIARY
or
INTELLIGENCE SUMMARY.
(Erase heading not required.)

Instructions regarding War Diaries and Intelligence Summaries are contained in F. S. Regs., Part II. and the Staff Manual respectively. Title pages will be prepared in manuscript.

Place	Date	Hour	Summary of Events and Information	Remarks and references to Appendices
	24.9.15		Transport & Machine Gun Section of Battalion left ALDERSHOT under the command of Major A. Y. S. Caldwell. They proceeded to SOUTHAMPTON & reached HAVRE that night. They entrained at HAVRE on Sunday at 10am & reached LILLERS Monday morning (27.9.15)	
	25.9.15		Remainder of the Battalion left ALDERSHOT & proceeded by train to FOLKESTONE. Crossed from FOLKESTONE and reached BOULOGNE early morning 26th.	
	26.9.15		The whole of this day was spent at OSTROHOVE REST CAMP BOULOGNE	
	27.9.15		The Battalion entrained at BOULOGNE & proceeded to march from LILLERS to LES HARISOIR on ordered to march from this day. The Transport horses were expecting to meet the Transport etc there to be BERGUETTE. The Destination of the Battalion was supposed to this station had they received BERGUETTE they might have been involved in the heavy fighting then in progress around HAZEBROUCK. On arrival at HAZEBROUCK instructions were received to detrain at CAESTRE. This was done & orders were then received to spend the night in billets at STRAZEELE which was subsequently altered to ROUGE CROIX a small village between CAESTRE and STRAZEELE.	
	28.9.15		The Evening of the 27th & morning of the 28th were spent in billets at ROUGE CROIX - orders were however received about 11:30 am to march to BAILLEUL at one o'clock. The 9th Loyal N. Lancs also marched to BAILLEUL	

Army Form C. 2118.

WAR DIARY
or
INTELLIGENCE SUMMARY.
(Erase heading not required.)

Instructions regarding War Diaries and Intelligence Summaries are contained in F. S. Regs., Part II. and the Staff Manual respectively. Title pages will be prepared in manuscript.

Place	Date	Hour	Summary of Events and Information	Remarks and references to Appendices
	29.9.15		While the other 2 Battalions of the Brigade were sent by Motors to ARMENTIÈRES the Battalion spent the night of the 28th at BAILLEUL, while Major Caldwell's party arrived at LE SAR the same night.	
		About 10.30 a.m.	About 10.30 a.m. the following morning the Battalion marched to ARMENTIÈRES acting on orders received from Brigade H/Q. The distance was about 10 miles & the weather was bad in addition to the men being heavily laden: only one man fell out this being the first case of a man having fallen out since the Battalion left ALDERSHOT. ARMENTIÈRES was reached about 1.30 p.m. & here the Battalion was joined by the Transport & Machine Gun Section.	
	30.9.15		The Battalion was attached to the 149th Brigade (50th Division) for instruction from this date to the 6th October.	
	6.10.15		By the 6th October the Battalion was ordered to move into billets at LE BIZET on the outskirts of ARMENTIÈRES the 9th Loyal N. Lancs Regt. it formed the Reserve for while together with the remaining 2 Battalions had previously occupied a line of trenches in front of LE BIZET on the evening of Sunday 3rd. On the 6th Oct the first casualty in the Battalion was reported: Pte Flanagan of "B" Coy while in the trenches for instruction being on morning was shot through the head & subsequently died in Hospital.	

2353 Wt. W2541/1454 700,000 5/15 D. D. & L. A.D.S.S./Forms/C. 2118.

WAR DIARY or INTELLIGENCE SUMMARY

Army Form C. 2118.

Place	Date	Hour	Summary of Events and Information	Remarks and references to Appendices
	7.10.15		From the 7th to the 12th was spent in Reserve Billets at LE BIZET. Companies were employed with the R.E. in digging communication trenches & in improving the subsidiary lines, which is manned by the Battalions in reserve in case of attack.	
	11.10.15		The Battalion manned the subsidiary line for instructional purposes. All was received at 6.30 pm and the men were got out by them.	
	12.10.15		The Battalion relieved the 13th Cheshires in the trenches on the evening of the 12th. The relief was successfully carried out by 7.30 pm.	
	13.10.15		A vigorous bombardment by our guns took place. There was in connection with events in other parts of the line: it was intended to destroy the enemy's wire and parapets as far as possible. Bombardment continued from 2 pm until about 5 pm. Enemy's wire cut in several places. Our parapets were not much damaged. The only considerable case was a gap of 6 ft. in C Coys lines. Little to report. Desultory shelling & sniping on the part of the enemy.	
	14.10.15			
	15.10.15		Very quiet during the day. In the evening a 'Sap' was believed to have been located opposite 'B' Company's trenches. Sappers & Brigade mining section assisted in the investigation but no definite conclusion arrived at.	

WAR DIARY
or
INTELLIGENCE SUMMARY.
(Erase heading not required.)

Army Form C. 2118.

Instructions regarding War Diaries and Intelligence Summaries are contained in F.S. Regs., Part II. and the Staff Manual respectively. Title pages will be prepared in manuscript.

Place	Date	Hour	Summary of Events and Information	Remarks and references to Appendices
	16.10.15		Noise heard again which gave rise to suspicion of "Sapping" – a trench was begun in front of our lines in order to cut in to see if there should prove to be one. A patrol taken out by Lt. Jones heard sounds of working underground.	
	17.10.15		The enemy shelled our trenches with 4.2 Howitzers. One shell fell 70 yards from Battn. Headquarters.	
	18.10.15		Our Machine Guns did good work on the enemy's working parties in the right on the right of trench 92. Several whistle blasts were heard, which probably denoted casualties.	
	20.10.15		The Battn. was relieved by the 13th Cheshires, and went into billets at LE BIZET till 26th inst., as 7th Brigade reserve.	
	22.10.15		Between 3 and 4 pm, the enemy's guns shelled the baths in LE BIZET with 6 inch High Explosive howitzer shells. Several shells fell through the roof of the baths. The Battn. suffered no casualties, as the men were quickly got into shell slits. One man of the 13th Cheshire Machine gun was hit in the arm. In consequence of the "strafe", the baths were closed down, which caused	W.M.

2353 Wt. W2514/1454 70C,000 5/15 D, D, & L. A.D.S.S./Forms/C. 2118.

WAR DIARY
or
INTELLIGENCE SUMMARY.
(Erase heading not required.)

Army Form C. 2118.

Place	Date	Hour	Summary of Events and Information	Remarks and references to Appendices
	26.10.15		as a little inconvenience to the baths and Batt. H.Q.R.S. were one and the same building. The 8th Loyal N. Lancs Regt was transferred from the 74th INF. BDE to the 7th INF. BDE. We relieved the 14th D.L.I. in PLOEGSTEERT WOOD. We found the trenches 121 to 123 in PLOEGSTEERT WOOD in rather a bad state of repair. Trenches very muddy and in rather a bad condition. Enemy aircraft showed activity over our line during the morning. Our anti-aircraft guns drove them away.	
	27.10.15		A patrol under 2nd Lt. MOIR D. Coy. went out and found our wire is rather a bad condition, some heads were seen over the "BOSCH" parapet wearing the Marine head dress. About 10.A.M. an enemy air-plane was brought down in our lines. Important information was gained from papers.	W.W.

Army Form C. 2118.

WAR DIARY
or
INTELLIGENCE SUMMARY.
(Erase heading not required.)

Place	Date	Hour	Summary of Events and Information	Remarks and references to Appendices
	28.10.15		The WORCESTER Regt on our left had a patrol in BROKEN TREE FARM which was set on fire by a German very light. The patrol had to return under rifle fire. Our machine guns swept the Bosch parapet, and stopped the nuisance effectively.	
	29.10.15		The enemy shelled the "STRAND" communication trench which leads through "PLOEGSTEERT WOOD". This was stopped by two "salvos" from our guns. In our trenches, some old trench boards were dug up from 6 or 8 inches deep and relaid.	
	30.10.15		From 9AM to 10.30 AM the enemy shelled MOAT FARM, held by C. Coy 2/L.N.L Regt. The Battn suffered no casualty, but a working party of the S.W.B. pioneer Battn had two men hit. One died during the day.	

W.W.

Place	Date	Hour	Summary of Events and Information	Remarks and references to Appendices
	30/10/15		A spy was suspected of being in ST. YVES AVENUE last night at 7.30 pm. A search was made without results. So far the Battn has been lucky with regard casualties. 2 killed and 9 wounded. Pte L. GREENHALGH. 15683 D. Coy killed in action and buried at the CEMETERY in "PLOEGSTEERT WOOD".	E.E.R
	31/10/15		Capt. H.F. GUIMARAENS, suffered bad bruising and possible internal injuries from his dug out falling in on him at 4.30 A.M. I was 2nd Lt. P. WALSH suffering from slight prix absence of the left temple caused by a fragment of a bullet. During the last six days, eighty Patrols and wiring parties have been out. No important information was gained. Extract from Battn orders of 30.9.15. "The Commanding Officer, Lieut - Col. W.H. Biddulph complemented the Battn on its high standard of discipline in arms reviewed since	W.W.

WAR DIARY
or
INTELLIGENCE SUMMARY.

(Erase heading not required.)

Army Form C. 2118.

handed over Command of the Battn.

COMPLIMENTARY.

"On the departure of the 8th Battn. Loyal N. Lancs Regt. to join the 4th INF BRDE. the G.O.C. (4th "B" BDE) desires to place on record his appreciation of the good work all ranks have performed since the raising of the Battn. He is sure that the Battn will under all circumstances uphold the traditions and reputation of the noted Regt. to which they belong, and in saying farewell he wishes officers, N.C.Os, and men all good fortune in the future."

W.T. Bidwell
LIEUT. COLONEL
COMMANDING 8th LOYAL NORTH LANCASHIRE REGT.

ORDERLY ROOM
3 NOV. 1915
8th (Ser) Bn. Loyal North Lancs. Regt.

25th Hussars
7th Bde

Pte A. W. Lanes
Vol 2
121/7656

Nov 15
6
22.22

2

Confidential

War Diary
of
8th. (Ser.) Battn Loyal North Lanc. Regt.
from Nov. 1 - 30   1915

Volume. 2

Place	Date	Hour	Summary of Events and Information	Remarks and references to Appendices
	Nov. 1		The Battalion was relieved in the trenches by the 1st Wilts Regt. The relief was carried out satisfactorily & the Battalion went into billets at THE PIGGERIES, PLOEGSTEERT. The place is where the name implies but is not used for keeping pigs any longer & makes quite comfortable billets. D Company was in tents and C Company occupied the subsidiary line B forts which are always occupied by one company. B The Battalion sen Brigade Reserve. The time during which the Battalion was in billet was busy occupied in making, digging, parties for work on communication trenches etc. Nothing of any importance occurred during this time	
	Nov. 2		Most of the Battalion except C Company managed to get baths which is out of the trenches. It is hoped that by next time the baths will be in full working order in that every man will be able to have a bath once a week. Item out of the trenches. On Nov 4 Lt WALSH rejoined the Battalion having escaped from Holland. The Battalion again went into the trenches, relieving the 1st Wilts. The relief was completed without mishap. The day passes quietly on the whole with the exception of 4 WHIZZ BANGS which landed	

WAR DIARY
or
INTELLIGENCE SUMMARY.
(Erase heading not required.)

Army Form C. 2118.

Place	Date	Hour	Summary of Events and Information	Remarks and references to Appendices
Somewhere near MOATED FARM	Nov. 8		occupied by a platoon of B Coy. No damage done by any bombardment. 1765 Pte KNOWLES 'D' Coy was shot through the head this day and was buried in the cemetery PLOEGSTEERT WOOD (Sh.L 28 U.21 c.4.5). During the day our snipers acting under Lt TONG's account 4 German snipers & dealt with them. 2 we know to have been hit. The others & closer firing. Our patrols had nothing to report of the enemy but troops took careful information of the conditions of the ground and of the enemy's wire.	
	Nov. 9		Enemy artillery fairly active during morning. Company working parties to stop work & take cover. They struck our parapet nice of places but did no considerable damage. Our artillery shelled the in the afternoon assisted by a trench mortar in an effort to destroy a suspected German machine gun emplacement. A good deal of damage was done in the night by gun fire to both to the fire trench parapet & communication trench as...	

WAR DIARY
or
INTELLIGENCE SUMMARY

Army Form C. 2118.

Place	Date	Hour	Summary of Events and Information	Remarks and references to Appendices
	10th – 12th Nov.		Little of note occurred. Our snipers are now becoming to learn their work fairly well and a considerable reduction in the German snipers activity has been noticeable lately.	
	12th Nov. 13th Nov.		No 1447/6 Pte J SEFTON of the Machine Gun Section was shot through the head & died in the Battalion was relieved by 1st Wilts & went into Divisional Reserve at PAPOT. This is a small village not far from Divisional Headquarters at NIEPPE. The men were mostly in huts & a barn though one Company was in tents. The whole place was very muddy. During the time at PAPOT the Battalion was occupied as before in providing digging parties to support and drain communication trenches & did not get much rest till except on the 14th which happened to be a Sunday.	Travel in PLOEGSTEERT WOOD
	17th		On the night of the 17th the Canadian Division on our left carried out a vigorous bombardment of the Enemy trenches. They followed this up by making a rush of 2 parties of about 25 men. One of these parties met with D/Bienstri & could not get forward. The other however reached the enemys trenches & (bayonets)	

WAR DIARY
or
INTELLIGENCE SUMMARY.
(Erase heading not required.)

Army Form C. 2118.

Place	Date	Hour	Summary of Events and Information	Remarks and references to Appendices
	19th Nov.		Some 30 Germans in addition to making 10 prisoners they only lost one killed & one wounded themselves	
	20th Nov.		The Battalion again came into the lt trenches, the relief being carried out successfully	
	21st Nov.		Little or nothing of note to report. Except a useful reconnaissance by 2/Lt RAMSAY Grenadier Officer, who penetrated to wire cables occupied by enemy on the right ⊕ of our line. Lt RAMSAY approached near enough to their sentry posts to hear them talking. Enemy wire regained some useful information as to their sentry posts.	
	22nd Nov.		2/Lt HOWARD made a good reconnaissance. He and his party proceeded up an old ditch alongside a hedge enemy straight out to our front. He then examined the German wire & succeeded in cutting it & bringing back a specimen. 2nd Return of patrol one man was found to be missing. The whole party volunteered to go out & bring him in though it was then bright moonlight & the enemy trenches only a little more than 100 yards distant, just as the party was preparing to go out again however the missing man came in unhurt.	
	23rd Nov.		2 Lt RAMSAY was wounded. Being shot through the right arm while outside the CRATERS filching a wiring party. This piece of ill luck is only attribut. 30 yards from the trenches.	

2353 Wt. W2541/1434 700,000 5/15 D. D. & L. A.D.S.S./Forms/C. 2118.

Army Form C. 2118.

WAR DIARY
or
INTELLIGENCE SUMMARY.
(Erase heading not required.)

Place	Date	Hour	Summary of Events and Information	Remarks and references to Appendices
	24.11.15		The Battalion was relieved by Wilts & went into billets at the PIGGERIES. Nothing of note occured during the time in billets - the usual working parties & fatigues were provided. One company was still in tents - but it is hoped that by the hut time the Battalion goes into billets huts will be ready. It is also hoped to have a recreation hut. A canteen (Reg'l Inst) was successfully started	
	29.11.15		The Battalion again went into the trenches - The relief was carried out successfully. Tours of duty in the trenches are now reduced to 5 days. Owing to the cold weather	
	30.11.15		Enemy showed considerably more activity in shelling. As a result we had 4 casualties (wounded) - 16819 Pte Ham - 15908 Pte Horocks - 17364 Pte Winsor - 15725 Pte Harris. During the month the weather has at times been very trying but the Battalion is to be congratulated on a very low percentage of men going sick.	

ORDERLY ROOM
1 DEC 1915
8th (Ser) Bn. Loyal North Lancs. Regt.

W.H.Brackenbury
LIEUT. COLONEL.
COMMANDING 8th LOYAL NORTH LANCASHIRE REGT.

8th L. N. Lancs.
Vol: 3
December 1915

121/7931

25th /5/31

Confidential

War Diary

of

8th (S.) Battalion Loyal N. Lanc. Regt.

from Dec 1 - 31

Volume 3

WAR DIARY
or
INTELLIGENCE SUMMARY.

Army Form C. 2118.

ORDERLY ROOM
DEC. 1915
8th (Ser) Bn. Loyal North Lancs. Regt.

Place	Date	Hour	Summary of Events and Information	Remarks and references to Appendices
DECEMBER	1st		Today there was a more or less ruined though dangerous building in the enemy lines. Our howitzers opened a heavy fire between 2.30 and 3 p.m. and did much damage - among our guns firing was a 9.2" and a 12 inch gun. We suffered no casualties. The enemy not replying to any considerable extent	
	2nd		Lttle of note to report. Enemy apparently satisfied by yesterdays bombardment. 15725 Pte HARRIS & 16819 Pte HAM wounded on 30th Nov. (spelt) died of wounds the same day. Pte HARRIS was attached to the Brigade Intelligence Section & his loss will be greatly felt.	
	3rd		No unusual occurrence. The night was very wet with the result that parts of the parapet fell in. also several dug outs. Many of these could not be repaired before the battalion left the trenches	
	4th		The battalion was relieved from Trench duty by 1st WILTS and went into Divisional Reserve at PAPOT - the place is a veritable sea of mud & it is almost impossible to cope with it. All Huts however have now gone & the men are all in huts	

Army Form C. 2118.

WAR DIARY
or
INTELLIGENCE SUMMARY.
(Erase heading not required.)

Place	Date	Hour	Summary of Events and Information	Remarks and references to Appendices
	4th		No 13430 Pte LANGSHAW of his Battalion (attached 171st Tunnelling Coy was accidentally killed being knocked down by a motor lorry. He was buried on 6th inst in MAPLE CEMETERY, LE ROMARIN.	
	5th		No work was done by the Battalion apart from cleaning up the camps. Most of the men had baths at the Divisional Baths.	
	6th		Weather very bad which does not improve condition of camp.	
	7th		Billets at PAPOT and New Transport lines were inspected by General Sir Herbert PLUMER (commanding 2nd Army). General PLUMER expressed himself as particularly pleased with New Transport lines.	
	8th		A British aeroplane came down in large ploughed field near on billets. The pilot had been shot in the leg when over LILLE but was not seriously hurt.	
	9th		The Battalion again went into trenches relieving 1st WILTS relief carried out successfully.	
	10th		Trenches are in a very bad condition owing to heavy rain and will need much work.	

Army Form C. 2118.

WAR DIARY
or
INTELLIGENCE SUMMARY.
(Erase heading not required.)

Instructions regarding War Diaries and Intelligence Summaries are contained in F.S. Regs., Part II. and the Staff Manual respectively. Title pages will be prepared in manuscript.

Place	Date	Hour	Summary of Events and Information	Remarks and references to Appendices
	11th		The Bad weather continues but the trenches are it would appear better than those of the rest of the Division at present. A message was received from G.O.C. 74th Brigade calling attention to a good piece of work by 13431 Corpl. Mc Cullough of this Regiment in charge of Salvage Section 74th Brigade. A house was set on fire by a shell in ARMENTIÈRES and a woman was left inside the burning building. Corporal Mc Cullough who was there at the time dashing into the building & rescued the woman. This act was brought to the notice of G.O.C. 7th Brigade who published a special order. (attached)	
	12th		The enemy shelled our sector to some extent; but our guns retaliated with about 10 shells to their one. No 14014 Pte MAGUIRE 'B' Coy received a serious bullet wound, the bullet passing through his lung. He died the same day in Field Ambulance. Lt. JONES was slightly wounded by a fragment thrown up by a rifle bullet. It is hoped that he will be back at duty quite shortly.	
	13th		Lt Jones returned to duty on the evening of 12th after an anti-tetanic injection — very little the worse for his wound	

Place	Date	Hour	Summary of Events and Information	Remarks and references to Appendices
	14th		The Battalion was relieved by 1st Wilts & went into BRIGADE RESERVE at the PIGGERIES.	
	15th		On the evening of 14th and early morning of 15th our batteries showed some activity and the German guns replied with about 30 rounds which passed over the PIGGERIES	
	16th		Battalion employed on working parties as usual. Nothing of note to report.	
	17th		The C.O. held a parade of the battalion in order to congratulate Capt McCullough on his act of gallantry.	
	19th		The battalion again went into the trenches relieving the 1st Wilts and Divisional Cyclists. Relief carried out without mishap. 1 company of the H.A.C. are attached to 1st WILTS for 15 days instruction. News was received on 19th of a gas attack made by the Germans in the early morning of that day on front between VERLORENHOEK and the YSER CANAL. The attack was quite unsuccessful	

Army Form C. 2118.

WAR DIARY
or
INTELLIGENCE SUMMARY.
(Erase heading not required.)

Place	Date	Hour	Summary of Events and Information	Remarks and references to Appendices
	20th		The day was quiet with no unusual occurrence	
	21st		2 Lt Howard was slightly wounded owing to his principle being smashed by an enemy sniper. He was struck by a piece of the glass which cut his head. He returned to duty however after an anti tetanic injection	
	22nd		In the early morning of the 22nd No 15690 Pte BAINES was shot through the head & died half an hour afterwards. He was buried the same day in PLOEGSTEERT WOOD CEMETERY	
	23rd			
	24th		The battalion was relieved by the WILTS and went into Divisional Reserve at PAPOT. The conditions here are very bad - the mud being to the most part knee deep. A certain amount of duck walks have been put down but we need many more.	
	25th		CHRISTMAS DAY. It was not easy to do anything in the way of celebrating Christmas. The men however were given a good dinner & tea with free beer. The battalion is very grateful to the people at home for all the things they sent out in the way of plum puddings, other food, tobacco. In the evening	

Army Form C. 2118.

WAR DIARY
or
INTELLIGENCE SUMMARY.
(Erase heading not required.)

Place	Date	Hour	Summary of Events and Information	Remarks and references to Appendices
	26th		A concert was held in a large barn in the farm. We were unable to get a piano but all things considered the concert was quite a success. A telegram of good wishes from Lt Col BIDDULPH (away on leave) was received. Similar telegrams were received from 2nd Corps - 25th Division - 7th Brigade - 1st Wilts - 9th Loyal North Lancs. Passed quietly without any notable occurrence - men were engaged on usual fatigues & in working on the drainage of the camp.	
	27th 28th		Nothing of note to report	
PLOEGSTEERT WOOD	29th		The Battalion relieved 1st Wilts in the trenches 16533 Pte CLEMMETT P. (B Coy) was killed by a bullet through the head. He was buried in STRAND cemetery	

2353 Wt. W254t/1454 700,000 5/15 D.D. & L. A.D.S.S./Forms/C. 2118.

WAR DIARY
or
INTELLIGENCE SUMMARY.

(Erase heading not required.)

Army Form C. 2118.

Place	Date	Hour	Summary of Events and Information	Remarks and references to Appendices
	30th		The Germans shelled the Right of our line and FORT BOYD considerably. One shell landed on a dug out in No 1 Post STRAND and killed 3 men 15622 Pte T. HASLAM. 15122 Pte R. ARNOLD 17541 Pte W. STONES. These were all buried in PLOEGSTEERT WOOD Cemetery (STRAND) A/C WILLIAMSON had a very lucky escape being only wounded.	
	31st		No 16191 L/Sgt. KAY was shot through the head by a sniper while driving some cattle round trenches. They were all looking over the parapet at the time. He was buried in PLOEGSTEERT WOOD. The New Year was ushered in by ourselves & the Germans with sharp rifle & M/gun fire & some fire from guns.	

W.M. Warwick
LIEUT. COLONEL,
COMMANDING 8th LOYAL NORTH LANCASHIRE REGT.

ORDERLY ROOM
31 DEC. 1915
8th (Ser) Bn. Loyal North Lancs.

--: 8TH (SERVICE) BATTALION LOYAL NORTH LANCASHIRE REGIMENT :--

C O P Y.

ROUTINE ORDERS.

BY

BRIGADIER GENERAL CMDG 7TH INFANTRY BRIGADE.

12 : 12 : 15

1. <u>SPECIAL ORDER.</u> The Brigadier has great pleasure is publishing the following for general information:-

On 9th inst, during a heavy bombardment, a house was set on fire in ARMENTIERES. A woman was wounded and lying hepp--less in the burning house, and was rescued by Corpl. McCullough, 8th Battn Loyal North Lancashire Regiment., who dashed into the house andbrought her out.

This gallant act on the part of Corpl. McCullough redounds to the credit of the Battalion to which he belongs.

(Signed) S.A.GABB, Captain.

Staff Captain, 7th Infantry Brigade.

7th INFANTRY BRIGADE ORDER NO. 6

The following instructions regarding the attitude to be adopted by the 7th Brigade towards the enemy on Christmas day are to be communicated to all ranks.

1. There is to be no fraternizing with the enemy of any sort.

2. We are at war with the enemy with the intention to kill whenever we have an oppertunity.

   No such oppertunity afforded by the enemy exposing himself is to be missed.

3. There will be no attempt at any organized Straaf on the enemy on Christmas day, except as retaliation.

4. Work will be continued as usual.

5. No precautions will be neglected on Xmas eve and Xmas night.

23/12/15.

L. P. Thomas, Major.
Bde Major, 7th Inf Bde.

7th INFANTRY BDE.
25th DIVISION.

8th BATTALION.

LOYAL NORTH LANCASHIRE REGIMENT

JANUARY 1916

Confidential

War Diary

of

8th (Ser) Battn Loyal North Lancashire Regt

From 1st January 1916 To 31st January 1916

(Volume No 4)

ORDERLY ROOM
1 - FEB 1916
8th (Ser) Bn. Loyal North Lancs. Regt.

Original

Army Form C. 2118.

WAR DIARY
or
INTELLIGENCE SUMMARY.
(Erase heading not required.)

Instructions regarding War Diaries and Intelligence Summaries are contained in F.S. Regs., Part II. and the Staff Manual respectively. Title pages will be prepared in manuscript.

Place	Date	Hour	Summary of Events and Information	Remarks and references to Appendices
1st			Enemy on the whole were quiet. Patrols were sent out in the evening; the conduct of L/Cpl SEED (B Coy) on this occasion is deserving of mention. An officer took a wiring party out at 4.15 am and had to withdraw after 20 minutes owing to rifle and machine gun fire. After getting the party safely back he sent Pte LEYLAND to warn the covering party to withdraw. "Verey lights" went up and machine gun fire opened and he crawled back. Pte MURRAY of the covering party was also hit by m/gun fire. L/Cpl. McNULTY who was in charge of this party sent the news to the office. Cpl. SEED on his own initiative went back with Pte HOLLINS and JONES under considerable fire and carried Pte MURRAY in, who in the second time Cpl. SEED has brought in a wounded man under similar circumstances, and the matter has been brought to the notice of G.O.C. 7th Infantry Brigade.	
2nd				
3rd			The Battalion was relieved by 1st Wilts & went into Brigade Reserve at PIGGERIES. On the morning of this day the enemy continued to English.	

Army Form C. 2118.

WAR DIARY
or
INTELLIGENCE SUMMARY.
(Erase heading not required.)

Place	Date	Hour	Summary of Events and Information	Remarks and references to Appendices
			Our Trench No 123 (held by A Coy) who Whizz bangs from Birichpu	
			MESSINES. No 15477 Sgt BUNYAN was hit & today wounded	
			He died the same afternoon in Field Ambulance & was buried	
			in ROMARIN CEMETERY PLOEGSTEERT.	
	4th		We bombarded the Enemy's front line with trench mortars & rifle	
			guns. There was no great retaliation though he keeping (our	
			occupied by Wilts) were damaged to a certain extent.	
			Our usual working parties etc were found by the battalion (chiefly	
	5th		for night work). All the new managed to have baths	
	6th		and change of clothes.	
			The Battalion again went into the trenches – a day earlier	
	7th		than was expected. Relief carried out successfully.	
			The enemy were quiet on the whole though they dropped some	
	8th		shells near Trench no 3 & also shelled parts of PLOEGSTEERT	
			WOOD	
			Between 10 and 10.30 AM the enemy sent about 40 "WHIZZ BANGS" on to ST	
	9th		YVES AVENUE and T123 from the direction of DEULEMONT. ST YVES AV.	

WAR DIARY
or
INTELLIGENCE SUMMARY.
(Erase heading not required.)

Army Form C. 2118.

Place	Date	Hour	Summary of Events and Information	Remarks and references to Appendices
PLOEGSTEERT WOOD			was badly knocked about and we had the misfortune to lose CAPTAIN CLARK, 15 Co. HQ of the Left Sect. (Hadley C Coy.) He was buried by a still shell which entered his H.Q.	
	10th	9.30AM 1.145PM 3.50PM	Heavy mortar was dropped on T123 morning and afternoon and midday West of STRAND. In all over 110" Bn RFA gun fired and attempts at retaliation met little success.	
		4.25PM	During afternoon heat in PLOEGSTEERT occupied by BDE. Bivouac was shelled analysing following casualties. Pte HEYES 4250 and BURNS 1550 wounded and Pte LITTLE 1550 & KILLED. The last named was buried by Brigade in cemetery at V25 c. b.1. ST.YVES	
	11th	9.45AM	The enemy dropped 42" WHIZZ-BANGS & 22 heavy HOWITZER shells on night of T123, ST.YVES, and LONE HOUSE, causing NO casualties and material damage. The howitzing its HOW. battery is unknown but the WHIZZ-BANGS are believed to have come from V16a 25.5. [?] these HOW. shells was dropped on E. end of ST.YVES at midnight. Very effective and adequate retaliation lasting throughout the morning was given by our artillery, who placed over a quantity of heavy stuff in the afternoon. In the evening considerable fire from a number of batteries, heavies and German trench mortars was experienced by our garrison. It's day, inferring enemy casualties.	
	12th	3.30PM	Enemy fired about 15 shells in vicinity of FORT BOYD. Between 6.30 & 7.30 pm over 200 shells (including about 30 small CRUMPS) were fired over FORT BOYD WESTMINSTER AV. HUNTERS AV. T123 & S1. Adequate retaliation was given by our guns. We had no casualties.	
	13th		Relieved by 1/WILTS Divisional Cyclists and went into Divisional Reserve at PAPOT: Relief	

WAR DIARY
or
INTELLIGENCE SUMMARY.
(Erase heading not required.)

Army Form C. 2118.

Place	Date	Hour	Summary of Events and Information	Remarks and references to Appendices
	14th 15th 16th 17th 18th		Carried out without mishap or casualty. The usual working parties were sent off daily. All men were provided with baths at Nutty eleven daily. Bombers being in workmens huts etc, were used voluntarily. A good deal of work was put in cleaning & laying down general improvements. On 14/17 another 50 men of the CONERAN and after 250 men of the ROADWELL arrived being attached to 2nd & PAPOT Battalions fulfilled. They were accommodated in the big barns and lofts generally used as dwellings.	
	19th		Battalion again went in to the trenches, relieving 1st WILTS on the afternoon of 19th. A gas attack was made by 74th Brigade on night of 8th on Divisional front. Our attack was successfully hit & was followed up by our own guns from our trenches in which 2nd R.I. RIFLES killed (it is believed) about 50 Germans & took about 10 prisoners. Our guns bombarded enemy trenches & were heavily shelling by enemy the day & there was some retaliation. About 12 heavy shells & some 20 WHIZZ BANGS fell in our own sector - no damage done.	
		7.0 p.m	Enemy was fairly quiet but alert & suspicious	

Army Form C. 2118.

WAR DIARY
or
INTELLIGENCE SUMMARY.
(Erase heading not required.)

Place	Date	Hour	Summary of Events and Information	Remarks and references to Appendices
21 SE			Enemy fairly quiet during day but at 8:45 pm they sent over 12 whizz bangs which landed in neighbourhood of Fort Boyd. One of these went through a dug out occupied by Grenadiers killing 2 men & wounding 2 others. 1 man in dug out escaped. Killed { 13738 - L/C Clegg W. 16507 Pte Bustard J.T. Wounded { 13651 Pte Almond W. 13703 Horsfall J.T. L/C Clegg & Pte Bustard are buried in Ploegsteert Wood cemetery	
22nd			No unusual occurrence	
23rd			Capt W. Furness was wounded in the early morning while out with a wiring party	
24th 25th			Battalion was relieved & went into Brigade Reserve at Piggeries. The Division being relieved by the 9th Division & going back into Corps Reserve. The Battalion marched to the area of La Creche & spent one night here in billets. The march was about 8 miles and considering the heavy loads	

WAR DIARY
or
INTELLIGENCE SUMMARY.
(Erase heading not required.)

Army Form C. 2118.

Place	Date	Hour	Summary of Events and Information	Remarks and references to Appendices
	25th		Which the men had to carry & the fact that they had just spent 4 months in the trenches with little marching, it is very creditable that no one fell out on the march.	
	26th		The Battalion marched off at 9 AM and arrived at its final destination near OUTTERSTEENE shortly before 11 AM. The billets have one very scattered but the men are comfortable.	
	27th 28th 29th 30th		The first 4 days are spent in resting & refitting before beginning Divisional training. The Division are organising a football competition for the best Company team in the Division.	
	31st		Work was started by the Battalion - 4 hours work a day chiefly close order drill & instruction of specialists	

K. M. Bremridge

LIEUT. COLONEL,
COMMANDING 8th LOYAL NORTH LANCASHIRE REGT.

ORDERLY ROOM
1 - FEB 1916
8th (Ser) Bn. Loyal North Lancs.

7th INFANTRY BDE.

25th DIVISION.

8th BATTALION.

LOYAL NORTH LANCASHIRE REGIMENT.

FEBRUARY 1916

Confidential

War Diary

8th Battn. Loyal North Lanc. Regt

From Feb 1 – 29   1916

Volume : 5

Army Form C. 2118.

WAR DIARY
or
INTELLIGENCE SUMMARY.
(Erase heading not required.)

8TH BN LOYAL NORTH LANCASHIRE REGT.

Place	Date	Hour	Summary of Events and Information	Remarks and references to Appendices
OUTTERSTEENE	Feb. 1st		The Battalion went into rest in the OUTTERSTEENE area on Jan. 26th. The last 4 days of the men were occupied in rifling and cleaning up generally. On the 1st Feb. training began. The work done was 4 hours a day in the morning: the men being free for football etc in the afternoons. For the first fortnight squad drill rifle exercises & Company drill formed the greater part of the work done. Later the men were practised in moving in extended order across country - and in the attack to formations which are easily forgotten in 4 months of trench warfare. An effort has been made to get as many men as possible trained in the use of grenades: Battalion classes lasting for 6 days, consisting of 12 men per company have been carried on by 2 Lt Ramsay. The battalion grenadier officer, and his instruction has also been carried out inside Company arrangements. Most of the men in the battalion have been	

Place	Date	Hour	Summary of Events and Information	Remarks and references to Appendices
	Feb 6-10		been given some instruction in the use of the LEWIS GUN. The 25th Division organised a football competition for the best company, battery, or other similar unit in the Division. Inter Company matches were played to decide the company which was to represent the battalion; and "B" Company was the winning company. Ours company however was unfortunately beaten by 3/D WORCESTERS in the inter battalion matches, after extra time.	
	Feb 9		On Feb. 9th the Brigade marched past the Army Commander (Gen Sir H. Plumer). The General complimented the battalion on the way in which the Transport was turned out.	
	Feb 14		Lt Col BIDDULPH left the battalion & proceeded to England Major CALDWELL taking over the command. Colonel BIDDULPH departure is greatly regretted by all ranks; he has commanded the battalion since the end of June 1915.	

Army Form C. 2118.

WAR DIARY
or
INTELLIGENCE SUMMARY.
(Erase heading not required.)

Place	Date	Hour	Summary of Events and Information	Remarks and references to Appendices

	Dec 8/15		A cross country race for teams of 10 from the various battalions etc of the Division was run. Although the team from this unit did not win the first man home was 19845 Pte CARSON "B" Coy. 8/L.N. Lancs. HEALTH OF BATTALION. The following figures were published by 25th Division from 1st October 1915 to 31st Jan. 1916 :—
			  8th L.N. Lancs 67
			  9th L.N. Lancs 104
			  8th S. Lancs 132
			  13th Cheshire 83
			  11th Cheshires 165
			  11th Lancs Fus 175
			  8th Borde Regt 180
			  10th Cheshire 228
			  6th S.D. & L. 255
			  2nd R.I. Rifles 140
			  13th Wilts Regt 170
			  3rd Worcesters 197
			  2nd S Lancers 225
				These figures are from 14 Oct 1915 only

Army Form C. 2118.

WAR DIARY
or
INTELLIGENCE SUMMARY.
(Erase heading not required.)

Place	Date	Hour	Summary of Events and Information	Remarks and references to Appendices
	Feb 13		The foregoing figures are certainly very conservative to this battalion. 2 new officers, 2 Lt SUMNER and 2 Lt BRUNKER, joined the battalion the former from the 3rd Battalion the latter from the 11th.	
	Feb. 16		About 8.0 AM a message was received from Brigade M/Q that the Brigade would proceed at once to ROMARIN to take up a position of readiness to reinforce the 2nd Corps. It was laid down that this battalion would form the starting point (about 30 minutes march from Batt. H/Q) at 11 AM. The battalion being billetted over a considerable area, this was short notice however was duly stocked in the apportioned places and the men turned out very quickly, the battalion as a result arrived at the starting point a quarter of an hour before time. The alarm proved to be a	

WAR DIARY
or
INTELLIGENCE SUMMARY.
(Erase heading not required.)

Army Form C. 2118.

Instructions regarding War Diaries and Intelligence Summaries are contained in F. S. Regs., Part II. and the Staff Manual respectively. Title pages will be prepared in manuscript.

Place	Date	Hour	Summary of Events and Information	Remarks and references to Appendices
	Feb 19		tell me & was only done for practice purposes. The result was very satisfactory.	
	Feb 20		News was received that Capt H.E. GUIMARAENS, on leave in England, had to undergo a serious operation. He will be away from the Battalion for at least 3 months. The Germans sent several hostile aeroplanes over our lines & dropped bombs on BAILLEUL causing about 30 casualties.	
	Feb 21		Capt BARNINGHAM was taken ill & had to go down to the base. It is believed that he is suffering from appendicitis.	
	Feb 22		A Brigade Field day took place: the 7th Bn were to attack the captains in front line & trenches were rather handicapped by the weather, there being a heavy snow storm on at the time.	

Army Form C. 2118.

WAR DIARY
or
INTELLIGENCE SUMMARY.
(Erase heading not required.)

Instructions regarding War Diaries and Intelligence Summaries are contained in F. S. Regs., Part II. and the Staff Manual respectively. Title pages will be prepared in manuscript.

Place	Date	Hour	Summary of Events and Information	Remarks and references to Appendices
	26th		The Division was warned to be ready to move at 9 hours notice by rail. It had been expected that the Division would move to ARMENTIERES to relieve the 21st Division this move however has been postponed.	
	27th		Major G. B. MARRIOTT (Royal Warwickshire Regt.) took over the command of his battalion.	
	28th) 29th)		nothing to record.	

G. B. Marriott Major
Cmdg 8th Bn LOYAL NORTH LANCASHIRE REGT.

ORDERLY ROOM
29 FEB. 1916
8th (Ser) Bn. Loyal North Lancs. Regt.

7th INFANTRY BDE.
25th DIVISION.

8th BATTALION.

LOYAL NORTH LANCASHIRE REGIMENT.

MARCH 1916

8 L.N Lancs Vol 6

Confidential

WAR DIARY

OF

8TH BN LOYAL NORTH LANCASHIRE REGT.

From 1st March to 31st March 1916

(VOLUME No. 6)

WAR DIARY or INTELLIGENCE SUMMARY

Army Form C. 2118.

Place	Date	Hour	Summary of Events and Information	Remarks and references to Appendices
OUTTERSTEENE	March 1st		Information was received that the move of the Division by rail was cancelled. It was stated that the Division would probably be here for another week and would then move by road.	
	2nd		Another practice alarm was carried out.	
		7.25 P.M.	Message received ordering battalion to pack up & get ready to move at once.	
		7.45 P.M.	Detailed orders followed his kindly. Battalion to be at cross roads METEREN by 9.30 P.M. It was stated that Brigade was moving to 'Eloperie 5th Corps.	
			All arrangements were carried out smoothly & satisfactorily and the battalion was at the 'rendezvous at the appointed time, though the notice given was very short.	
			The alarm was believed to be a real one, particularly in view of the news of brisk fighting at YPRES received during the day.	

Army Form C. 2118.

WAR DIARY
or
INTELLIGENCE SUMMARY.
(Erase heading not required.)

Instructions regarding War Diaries and Intelligence Summaries are contained in F. S. Regs., Part II. and the Staff Manual respectively. Title pages will be prepared in manuscript.

Place	Date	Hour	Summary of Events and Information	Remarks and references to Appendices
	3rd to 8th		Nothing to report. Usual work was carried out. The Division was standing by, ready to move at any time.	
		9h	Orders were received that the Brigade would move South on the following day.	
		10h	The Brigade marched out of OUTTERSTEENE area at 8 A.M. and marched 5- to the ROBECQUE area. Route followed was VIEUX BERQUIN — MERVILLE — CALONNE SUR LA LYS — ROBECQUE. This Battalion proceeded further through BUSNES and spent the night at LA PIERRIÈRE. Distance covered 17¼ miles. Only one man fell out to be picked up by Field Ambulance.	
LA PIERRIÈRE		11h	The Battalion marched off from LA PIERRIÈRE at 9 A.M. and passed the Brigade starting point at LILLERS CH. at 10.36 A.M. Route LILLERS — BURBURE — PERNES — TANGRY — HESTRUS, at which latter place the Battalion went in to Billets	
HESTRUS				

Army Form C. 2118.

WAR DIARY
or
INTELLIGENCE SUMMARY.
(Erase heading not required.)

Instructions regarding War Diaries and Intelligence Summaries are contained in F. S. Regs., Part II. and the Staff Manual respectively. Title pages will be prepared in manuscript.

Place	Date	Hour	Summary of Events and Information	Remarks and references to Appendices
	11/k		On this day also only one man fell out who did not rejoin the same day. This record is a very creditable one, the regiment having the smallest number of men who fell out in the Brigade.	
			Extract from Regimental Orders 11.3.16	
			"The Commanding Officer is greatly pleased at the excellent spirit displayed by the all ranks during two long and trying marches, and congratulates the battalion on the very small percentage of men who fell out."	
			Farewell order by IInd Corps Commander - circulated under 25th Divl. R.O. 794 of 10.3.16	
			"On the departure of the Division from the 2nd Corps, I would like to express my great regret at the severance of our connexion, and my sincere congratulations and thanks for all the good work that the Division has done during the last six months.	

Army Form C. 2118.

WAR DIARY
or
INTELLIGENCE SUMMARY.
(Erase heading not required.)

Place	Date	Hour	Summary of Events and Information	Remarks and references to Appendices
			Farewell order (continued)	
			"Commanders of all grades, Staffs and Units have worked most loyally and whole-heartedly; and I know that they will keep up the reputation which the Division has already made for itself. I wish the Division the best of luck and success in the future."	
	12th		Sunday was spent in resting and no work was done. The battalion still remained at HESTRUS. Company training being carried out.	
	13th			
	14th		A short battalion route march took place the equipment being worn for its long marches.	
	15th		On the evening of the 14th orders were received to move to MAIZIÈRES a place about 12 miles further South. The battalion marched via HUCLIER - BRYAS - MARQUAY - AVERDOINGT to MAIZIÈRES.	
MAIZIÈRES	16th		The battalion remained in billets at MAIZIÈRES where they are in Corps reserve. The other two Divisions	

Army Form C. 2118.

WAR DIARY
or
INTELLIGENCE SUMMARY.
(Erase heading not required.)

Place	Date	Hour	Summary of Events and Information	Remarks and references to Appendices
	16th		As the XVII th Corps having already gone in to the line it appeared probable that this Battalion would remain at MAIZIÈRES for about 3 weeks. Extract from Battalion Orders 18.3.1916 The Brigadier wishes it to be known by the Battalion that he is very pleased at the way in which they have performed their marches. The Battalion has marched better than any other in the Brigade. He is particularly pleased with those men who, though they had bad feet, stayed in the ranks in hand falling out. This he considers shows a proper spirit.	
16th to 29th		During the time when the Battalion was at MAIZIÈRES (using war Games) and on the same times as when in Corps Reserve at OUTTERSTEENE. Close order drill, bombing practice are being carried on Route marching	

2353 Wt. W2544/1454 700,000 5/15 D.D.&L. A.D.S.S./Form/C. 2118.

WAR DIARY
or
INTELLIGENCE SUMMARY.

Army Form C. 2118.

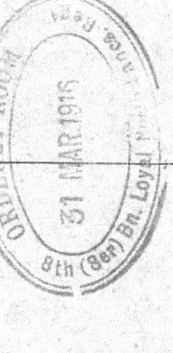

Place	Date	Hour	Summary of Events and Information	Remarks and references to Appendices
	16-24		An inter-platoon football tournament has been arranged. The winning platoon being No 3 Platoon	
	29		Two companies were ordered to proceed to MAROEUIL to carry materials for 51st Division. There 2 Coys under Command of Major CALDWELL left for MAIZIÈRES at 1pm 29.3.1916. The companies sent to MAROEUIL were "A" and "B" Coys.	
	31		The Battalion, less detachment at MAROEUIL, was inspected by the Commander in Chief (Gen. Sir DOUGLAS HAIG). The men were inspected in thrusting exercises & bayonet fighting.	

J.B. Howarth Major
O.C. 8TH BN LOYAL NORTH LANCASHIRE REGT.

7th INFANTRY BDE

25th DIVISION.

8th BATTALION.

LOYAL NORTH LANCASHIRE REGIMENT

APRIL 1916

U/38 L N Lancs
vol 7.

CONFIDENTIAL

WAR DIARY

of

8th Bn LOYAL NORTH LANCASHIRE REGT

From 1st April 1916
To 30th April 1916

(VOLUME 7.)

Army Form C. 2118.

WAR DIARY
or
INTELLIGENCE SUMMARY.
(Erase heading not required.)

Instructions regarding War Diaries and Intelligence Summaries are contained in F. S. Regs., Part II. and the Staff Manual respectively. Title pages will be prepared in manuscript.

Place	Date	Hour	Summary of Events and Information	Remarks and references to Appendices
MAIZIERES	April 2		Sports were organised by "C" Company. The heats being run on Sunday Ap. 2 & the finals on Monday Ap. 3. A concert was arranged for the evening which proved a great success.	
	5		A Brigade route march took place - the Brigade marched past the Corps Commander Lt. Gen. Sir Julian Byng.	
	6		Inter-Platoon Relay Races were held - each team consisting of 8 men - the distance being 500 yds. The Machine Gun Team won after a very close race - No 11 Platoon being second.	
	8		A Concert was given by "D" Company in the evening which was very successful.	
	11		"C" & "D" Companies together with Specialists move to huts area - "C" to ECOIVRES & "D" outside MAROEUIL.	

2353 Wt. W2514/1454 700,000 5/15 D. D. & L. A.D.S.S./Forms/C. 2118.

Army Form C. 2118.

WAR DIARY
or
INTELLIGENCE SUMMARY.
(Erase heading not required.)

Instructions regarding War Diaries and Intelligence Summaries are contained in F. S. Regs., Part II. and the Staff Manual respectively. Title pages will be prepared in manuscript.

Place	Date	Hour	Summary of Events and Information	Remarks and references to Appendices
MARDEUIL	12th to 20th		The Battalion remained in the MARDEUIL area working for the 51st Division. A.r.B. Coys being employed for carrying and C.D.Coys working on the Corps line.	
	20th		On the night of the 20th the Battalion went to the trenches in front of MONT ST ELOY relieving the 5th SHERWOOD FORESTERS 46th Division. The relief was carried out successfully. The condition of the trenches is in many places very bad here is very scanty dug out accommodation A great deal of work will have to be done on them.	
	21st to 23rd		The Battalion remained in the trenches for 3 days. On the night of the 22nd a German mine was exploded to the front of the greater part of the Battalion being "standing to" all the night. The water round being very bad indeed. The mine however was not exploded.	
	23rd	23.10	The Battalion was relieved by 1st Wilts on return of 23rd. The relief was carried out satisfactorily on Brigade Reserve at ST ELOY.	

2353 Wt. W25141/1452 700,000 5/15 D. D. & L. A.D.S.S./Forms/C. 2118.

WAR DIARY
or
INTELLIGENCE SUMMARY.

(Erase heading not required.)

Army Form C. 2118.

Place	Date	Hour	Summary of Events and Information	Remarks and references to Appendices
	23rd to 26th		The battalion only remained at MONT ST ELOY for 3 days; each company had to carry out one nights work in the forward system of trenches. On the evening of the 26th the Battalion again went in to the trenches relieving 1st. Wilts. Relief was carried out successfully.	
	27th		Day was fairly quiet except for a little sniping. During the morning the enemy subjected NEUVILLE-ST-VAAST on our Right to a heavy bombardment. A few shells fell in our area but no damage was done.	
	28	About 3.0 AM.	a mine was exploded some distance to the Right of our line - this was followed by an in tense bombardment - our artillery retaliated but did not appear to be able to bring back a heavy fire to bear on the Germans	

WAR DIARY
or
INTELLIGENCE SUMMARY.
(Erase heading not required.)

Army Form C. 2118.

Place	Date	Hour	Summary of Events and Information	Remarks and references to Appendices
	28		The day was quiet (except for the shelling of NEUVILLE ST VAAST about noon) until 7.30 PM when the enemy put up a mine on our left. The artillery on both sides opened a heavy fire until about 9.0 pm.	
	29		Day quiet until about 6.30 pm when we opened a heavy fire on the enemy trenches. Enemy retaliated with an intense fire. The 3/WORCS. on our left suffered much from his bombardment, comparatively few shells falling in our sector. About 8.15 pm & again at 9.0 am the 3/WORCESTERS attempted to recapture trench which had been taken the previous day & which was held by enemy. Both attempts were unfortunately unsuccessful.	
	30		Enemy showed no great activity, except between 6 & 7.30 pm when they opened intense bombardment on our right & left. Following mine explosions 2nd Lt MARSHALL was wounded in the leg by a bomb	fr./

WAR DIARY
or
INTELLIGENCE SUMMARY.

Carpathia in action during April.

Killed . 4
Wounded. 29 O.R 1 Officer
Accidentally Wounded 2 (one of whom died of wounds)

A.B. Maxwell
LIEUT. COLONEL,
COMMANDING 8th ROYAL NORTH LANCASHIRE REGT.

7th INFANTRY BDE.

25th DIVISION.T

8th BATTALION.

LOYAL NORTH LANCASHIRE REGIMENT

MAY 1916

CONFIDENTIAL

WAR DIARY

OF

8TH BN LOYAL NORTH LANCASHIRE REGT.

FROM:- 1ST MAY 1916 TO:- 31st MAY 1916

(VOLUME (8))

WAR DIARY
or
INTELLIGENCE SUMMARY.
(Erase heading not required.)

Army Form C. 2118.

Place	Date	Hour	Summary of Events and Information	Remarks and references to Appendices
	May			
	1		The day was quite normal — the enemy showed his usual activity except for small bombing encounters. A relief was arranged to have taken place in the Evening trenches.	
	2		Quiet during early part of the day — but about 7.30 pm just before the relief by 1/WILTS was due to begin the enemy put up a mine on our left & an intense artillery fire was opened by both sides. The relief was only delayed about an hour however & the early hours of the morning successfully completed by May 3.	
	3.		The Battalion went into Divisional Reserve — 3 Companies being at MONT ST. ELOY, and M/O, Specialists, & 1 Coy at ACQ.	
	4 to 8		The battalion was able to have a very good rest while in Divisional Reserve as they were not called upon to supply many working parties.	

Place	Date	Hour	Summary of Events and Information	Remarks and references to Appendices
	7 to 8		Nearly all the men managed to get a bath & a change of clothes.	
			On the night of the 8th the Battalion should have gone in to the trenches to relieve 1/WILTS - the relief however was postponed owing to the fact that it had been arranged to blow up one of our mines on the Brigade front	
		9th	The Battalion went into the trenches relieving 1st WILTS. Relief carried out successfully. Shortly before relief enemy exploded a mine in our line the men of the crater was successfully occupied by WILTS & consolidating work finished by us after relief	
		10th	Our day passed quietly except for a time rifle grenade firing on the left of our line.	
		11th	We have made considerable use of our STOKES GUN. There are found particularly effective when enemy's against are hit of a rifle grenade by the enemy. They certainly silence attempts at trombing & sniping	[i]

WAR DIARY
or
INTELLIGENCE SUMMARY
(Erase heading not required.)

Army Form C. 2118.

Place	Date	Hour	Summary of Events and Information	Remarks and references to Appendices
	12		It is suspected that a relief has taken place in the German line since the battalion was last in the line. One important group appears to be ranging on many of the important points in this area. A considerable number of heavy shells have fallen around Battn H/Q & the QUARRIES (the trench where H/Q is situated).	
	13th		Heavy rain during the night & up to mid-day has seriously tried the condition of the trenches very bad & has severely handicapped our work.	
	14th		About 7.30 pm the enemy threw trench mortar bombs in G on posts on ALBANY crater, killing one man & wounding 5, one of whom subsequently died of wounds.	
	15th		Enemy again used trench mortars without doing any damage. A relief is suspected to have taken place in enemy trenches. About 8.15 pm six mines were exploded in Brigade on our right. There was a strong artillery barrage which did considerable damage to the front trenches of this Bn garr-	

Army Form C. 2118.

WAR DIARY
or
INTELLIGENCE SUMMARY.
(Erase heading not required.)

Place	Date	Hour	Summary of Events and Information	Remarks and references to Appendices
	15th		Our own area was not greatly affected except for a certain amount of damage to front & trenches. Caused by enemy shelling. Enemy quiet except for a little trifling shelling and rifle grenading.	
	16th		Nothing unusual to report	
	17th 18th		On the evening of the 18th the Battalion was relieved by the WILTS & went into Brigade Reserve. The Battalion is not all together this time but is distributed over a large area in the subsidiary line system of trenches. Split up & extends over a large area in the subsidiary line system of trenches. During the relief there was an intense bombardment on our left, but it was chiefly restricted to the 74th Brigade & did not affect our relief.	
	18th		On the night of the 18/19 the Battalion clear in trench held by the Battalion on our left on our side of BROADMARSH crater.	

Army Form C. 2118.

WAR DIARY
or
INTELLIGENCE SUMMARY.
(Erase heading not required.)

Place	Date	Hour	Summary of Events and Information	Remarks and references to Appendices
		19h	This Battalion received orders from Brigade H/Q on the morning of the 19th inst. to provide 100 men for a counter attack to recapture his lost ground. The enterprise was organised & arranged by Major A.F.S. CALDWELL, men in command of the Battalion. Our guns kept up a continual fire on the Centre until 9.15 p.m at which time the attack was timed to take place. They then lifted and the attack began. Parties taking part in the operation. I 20 men under 2 Lt HOWARD. This party was equipped only with bayonets & bandoliers and with one bomb in each coat pocket. There duty was to crawl forward in 2 lines to within 30 yards of the enemy's a small distance apart to within 30 yards of the enemy's position; they were then to take the enemy's top surprise using their bayonets to full advantage; rifle fire and bombs being only used if absolutely necessary. II (a) A party of 20 men under 2 Lt TATAM. These were ordered to leave the front trench as soon as the first party charged & to carry up a good supply of	

WAR DIARY
or
INTELLIGENCE SUMMARY

Army Form C. 2118.

bombs & men were their equipment & carried 4 sandbags each in their belts to be ready to start the work of consolidating the captured position.

(b) A party of 10 men whose duty it was to keep up the supply of bombs by carrying them up a small trench running up to the right of the crater.

III. A party of 50 men under 2 N.C.O.'s who were to be kept in reserve, to be used to follow up and complete work of consolidation.

IV. A Lewis gun was to fire from a trench half way up the small communication trench running up to the right of the crater, the block divided the German position from our own.

The Attack.

The first party left our trench at 9.15 p.m. with great skill 2nd Lieut HOWARD led his men quite unobserved by the

2353 Wt. W2514/1454 700,000 5/15 D.D.&L. A.D.S.S./Forms/C. 2118.

Enemy to within 20 x of the German position & the Party then gave a cheer & charged 2 Lt HOWARD was wounded in the thigh by a bomb almost at once & Sergt. W. POWELL took charge of the party which successfully gained the rear lip of the crater & held it under heavy fire. Shortly afterwards 2 Lt WALSH came up from the rear & took charge of the trenches which he did with great skill & coolness.

The Germans in occupation of the crater took to their heels immediately our first party charged & were apparently completely surprised, since they left behind him a quantity of ammunition & rifles. They are believed to belong to a regiment of Guards.

As soon as the Germans became aware of our attack a terrific bombardment was opened on our trenches which continued with great intensity for about 3 hours. Fortunately we did not suffer greatly from this trench mortar.

Consolidation of position.

When the position was once gained we took up consolidation [?]

Army Form C. 2118.

WAR DIARY
or
INTELLIGENCE SUMMARY.
(Erase heading not required.)

Instructions regarding War Diaries and Intelligence Summaries are contained in F.S. Regs., Part II. and the Staff Manual respectively. Title pages will be prepared in manuscript.

Place	Date	Hour	Summary of Events and Information	Remarks and references to Appendices
			Began immediately - our men at the same time moving a continuous stream of trouts into the German trenches. In the early hours of the morning a party of "D" Coy under 2 Lt HENLEY relieved the original men who were domicilied & slaughter & carried on the work of consolidation. The following officers & N.C.Os deserve mention in connection with this operation. <u>2 Lt HOWARD.</u> For his skill in dealing the counter attack & also to the German lines without being observed <u>2 Lt WALSH.</u> To his conduct of affairs after 2 Lt HOWARD became a casualty; in this he showed great coolness & marked ability. He was working under a heavy fire all the time <u>2 Lt BARNINGHAM</u> also as organising officer made very efficient arrangements for communication to the result that his messages were transmitted & received throughout the operation & communication was never lost. He also deserves mention for his conduct of the trouts supply	

2353 Wt. W25H14454 700,000 5/15 D.D.&L. A.D.S.S./Forms/C. 2118.

Army Form C. 2118.

WAR DIARY
or
INTELLIGENCE SUMMARY.
(Erase heading not required.)

Place	Date	Hour	Summary of Events and Information	Remarks and references to Appendices
			Sgt. W. POWELL for great gallantry & skill in taking charge of a Lewis gun party after 2/Lt HOWARD had been wounded.	
			Capt. MARSDEN was himself wounded in 3 places continued to work his Lewis Gun.	
			Pte WILKINSON, who showed great courage in bringing in the wounded (among them 2/Lt HOWARD) under fire.	
	20731		Pte SWIFT. Who took charge of a Lewis Gun & continued pulling men together at a very critical moment.	
	16234		Pte HIFTON killed while carrying bombs to the open under heavy M/Gun fire.	
			All ranks worked extremely well & earned the praise of the Brigadier & the Divisional r Corps Commanders. The battalion may well be proud of the whole operation.	

WAR DIARY
or
INTELLIGENCE SUMMARY

Army Form C. 2118.

Place	Date	Hour	Summary of Events and Information	Remarks and references to Appendices
	21		Casualties We had the misfortune to lose 2 Lt L.C. TATAM early in the operation. It is not known how he was killed & his body has not yet been recovered. 2 Lt EDWARD was wounded by a bomb in the night & subsequently died of wounds in hospital. 2 Lt HENLEY was shot through the head by a German sniper while being relieved with his platoon of D Coy which had carried on the work of consolidating the crater. Casualties in other ranks. Killed 9. Wounded 18. Missing 4. During the 21st the enemy heavily bombarded the crater captured by us. No shells fell in the crater but the communication trench to BROADMARSH was heavily bombarded with trench mortars & in the evening about 6 pm was quite cut off by a curtain of gas shells. It was impossible for the limbs guns & the stretcher bearers to come up & all the troops at the front from trenches	

WAR DIARY or INTELLIGENCE SUMMARY

Army Form C. 2118.

(Erase heading not required.)

Summary of Events and Information

The trolly leaves were relayed. The men in the crate had no help from any Lewis Gun throughout the action.

Lt JONES who was in charge of 6.0 pm. r hold the men what round the posts at 6.0 pm. r hold the men that he expected the Germans would attack the crater from our W.O. Any arrangements were therefore made for covering the left flank of each bomb post of what mine crater. Due on the way from the but of our defences to such a 1 on the way from , 1 at the Eastern edge of half way to the bridge craters.

At about 7.30 pm. the Germans blew up a mine about 35 x 35. S. of BROADMARSH Crater & immediately attacked. This guns lifted from the first line trenches at the same hour.

The first line of their German attack was made with men at 3 x intervals, the succeeding lines being much heavier. In the 2nd & 3rd lines many men were seen carrying tools were r hinder to consolidate their position & its inflicted heavy casualties on the men trying up & more materials.

In the platoon were several exceptionally good bombers notably Pte REGAN who was able to reach the far edge of the newly formed crater

May 21. (contd)

from No 2 post he threw fifteen boxes of bombs. An attempt made to fit a machine gun in position by the Germans was frustrated, the gun being knocked out by one of our bombs. The tip of his rifle was kept clear of Germans for quite an hour by the bombers & snipers of Nos 3 & 4 posts. No 2 post containing 3 men faced right & left Pte Regan throwing to the right being covered by Ptes FINCH & LLOYD. The supply of bombs ran short & several men tried to get through to bring more up (notably L/c Hornby & Pte Meadows). But could find none. Finally when all the bombs were gone he men all used their rifles. Lt JONES lay near No 2 post calling out he had two craters he made him on Germans coming along between the two craters. By his side in the mud were 3 bombs. He picked up one and jumped up to throw when he was shot through the head & fell back dead. Sgt Sergt (Sgt GRAYSON) had been killed some time before & Mr command of his section fell on Capt. COATES who had been wounded some time previously in 4 places. He sat in the french chasing on his knees & killing men that seen for enemies were due to arrive. At the ammunition was now used up including that on dead men & some lying about in the trench. Finally he men threw lumps of chalk & flint & even empty bomb boxes. Their bayonet range and pictured L Minor.

The Germans never came within

May 31 (cont'd)

bombs & rifle grenades from a safe distance. In the end, nothing further being possible, the men decided to come out if possible across the open & make a bolt for it with the bayonet. No 1 post of which 3 men were still alive ran down after him but on the way one of them (Pte SANGSTER) a box of bombs trying on the edge of the parapet. They therefore stopped & threw these, & Pte ELKINS, one of them, said in his evidence "we left some of them to stay with Mr. TATAM" (Lt TATAM had been killed when we both the under on the 19th & his body had been lying in the open since then.) All those men got out finally & met, somewhere in the P. line Sgt. SIBBERING who had previously gone for bombs. with a Cheshire Sergeant These men built a barricade of sand bags & Pte SANGSTER remained with this Sergt. all night while the other two carries bombs for them under the command of a Cheshire Officer. They were all suffering split up. The original party was now completely. The Opinion of all the men from the gas shells. Some more than others. with them they could have is not of they could have had a davin gun "savage" that the between them of held out much longer. of course made to their credit that they made such a the position inevitable; it is greatly to their credit that they made such a fine resistance. Nine of the men returned unwounded (18.30), 14 wounded were brought out during the day. The final evacuation took place about 10.0 pm.

May 21 (combat)

It is difficult to emphasise any name in connection with the operation: all ranks from Lt. JONES throughout the platoon upheld the honours of the Battalion in a manner of which the whole Battalion is justly proud.

The German attack on BROADMARSH crater was only the left of a big attack along the whole front of the Brigade or our left. After an intense bombardment of about 5 hours the Germans attacked about 7.30 pm (as already stated). They broke through our outpost line, capturing No. 5 craters which had been held by 7th Brigade (how our B Bn line) & established themselves in the "P" line or line of resistance, occupied the "S" line also which is the outpost line.

About 9.30 pm the Battalion received orders to counter-attack on P. 78. 79. "S" line & having taken this to take the "B" line on the same frontage (about 300 x).

The only information to hand was that the Battalion on our left was holding OLD BOOT ST (a support trench running off CENTRAL the main communication trench on the left of on Frigade) & that blocked CENTRAL here. LASSALE (the communication trench on the right of CENTRAL) was in our possession & was blocked to the left & the Germans were holding the S line 78 & 79 with the exception of some 50 x on the right outposts & the held by a working party of our own. (This left in communication forward to

May 21 (contd)

be wrong, since the party had taken from their original position to the P line & helped the XI Cheshires to hold his during the night.

We were ordered to deploy in front of the line & SOMBARD, & small trench joining CENTRAL & LASSALE, & attack with the bayonet alone. The division on our left were to counter attack at 2 am.

Disposition
CENTRAL with orders to deploy to the right & get in touch with Capt Foote commanding A Coy : B Coy under Lt. Fish was on the right of A., with 2½ platoons D Coy on extreme right. Major Wynne (O.C. D Coy) was in charge of the whole line. Besides the looking party, men housed about 30 men of D Coy under Lt Jones were holding BROADMARSH CRATER.

May 22.

The deployment was complete at 1.45 am and the line advanced crawling. A heavy shelling of the position it had just left began when the line had gone some 50x and several men were hit by fragments of shell.

WAR DIARY
or
INTELLIGENCE SUMMARY

(Erase heading not required.)

Army Form C. 2118

When about 100 x from the S. line fire was opened on it by at least 2 machine guns. Major Wynne gave the order to advance at the double & after firing a few more bursts of fire from the machine gun & throwing some bombs the Germans bolted & were seen disappearing into the F line. As losses had been heavy & some men had been held up by wire on the right & also as there were no signs of any attack on our left Major Wynne decided to advance no further.

A strong party went up CAVALIER Trench & fired a Clock there about 50 x & another up CENTRAL which moved to within 30 x of the F line & found no Germans. To protect our left front CAVALIER was indeed disarranged & fire step made. Work was begun at once on the S line & the wires made fairly safe except for a break of about 60 x in the middle. The night passed quietly & good work could be done.

At 2.45 pm on 22nd inst some green lights were shot

Army Form C. 2118

WAR DIARY
or
INTELLIGENCE SUMMARY
(Erase heading not required.)

Place	Date	Hour	Summary of Events and Information	Remarks and references to Appendices
	May 23 to 28		Casualties for operation on night of 21st/22nd. OFFICERS Killed. Lt Jones, R.B.B. " Nicholls E.J. Wounded Capt Foot T.M. Lt Taylor L.T. Lt Gregory F. 2 Lt Bruger W.Y. " Muir R.D. " Whitehead W.J. Other Ranks Killed : 27 Wounded : 103 missing : 15 The battalion remained in dug outs in PYLONES and BETHUNE ROAD. Men were chiefly employed in doing night fatigues & in repairing damage done to left sector during recent operations.	

WAR DIARY
or
INTELLIGENCE SUMMARY
(Erase heading not required.)

Army Form C. 2118

Place	Date	Hour	Summary of Events and Information	Remarks and references to Appendices
	28		On the night of the 28th the battalion was relieved by 10th Cheshire R. in Brigade Reserve & went into billets at ACQ	
	29 to 31		Battalion was in billets at ACQ. all the men got baths, clean clothing & a much needed rest.	
	31st		The battalion marched to MONCHY BRETON in the left area, the whole division is now being in forces 8 being relieved	

7th Infg. Brigade

SPECIAL ORDER OF THE DAY

The following has been received from the Army Commander:—

Headquarters
27th May 1916.

The Army Commander has read with interest the account of the successful attack on the

Army Form C. 2118

WAR DIARY
or
INTELLIGENCE SUMMARY

(Erase heading not required.)

Place	Date	Hour	Summary of Events and Information	Remarks and references to Appendices
BROADMARSH			Raid by a party of the 8th Loyal North Lancashire Regiment on night of May 19/20. Please convey the Army Commander's congratulations to all troops who took part in the Operation.	

G.B. Manwaring
LIEUT. COLONEL
COMMANDING 8th LOYAL NORTH LANCASHIRE REGT.

ORDERLY ROOM
MAY 1916
8th (Ser) Bn. Loyal North Lancs. Regt.

7th INFANTRY BDE
25th DIVISION.

8th BATTALION.

LOYAL NORTH LANCASHIRE REGIMENT

JUNE 1916

LNL-W-1

From:- O Comdg 8th (S) Battn
Loyal North Lancs Regt
To:- D.A.Gs Office
3rd Echelon

Herewith War Diary for
month of June 1916-

5-7-16   R. B. Heawood
          Lieut Col
          Comdg 8th (S) Battn L.N.L Regt

8 L.N Lancs June
Vol 9

Confidential

XXV

WAR DIARY
of
8th (Ser) Batt Royal North Lancashire Reg

From 1st June To 30th June 1916

(VOLUME 9.)

ORIGINAL

Army Form C. 2118

WAR DIARY
or
INTELLIGENCE SUMMARY
(Erase heading not required.)

Place	Date	Hour	Summary of Events and Information	Remarks and references to Appendices
MONCHY BRETON	JUNE 1.		On the night of May 31 the Battalion marched to MONCHY BRETON from ACQ about 13½ miles. The Battalion left ACQ at 8.0 PM and arrived at MONCHY BRETON at 1.30 AM : only 2 men fell out both of whom rejoined. The whole Division is at present in Corps reserve : a complete and progressive system of training is laid down for a fortnight the men working from 6 to 8 hours a day. Battalion is considerably handicapped by a shortage of Officers & N.C.O.s owing to the recent operations : it is hoped however that a draft may be sent shortly.	
	3		Information was received that LT. L.T. TAYLOR had died of wounds received on the night of May 21. He died at No. 42 Casualty Clearing Station AUBIGNY & was buried at AUBIGNY 4.6.1916.	

WAR DIARY
or
INTELLIGENCE SUMMARY
(Erase heading not required.)

Army Form C. 2118

Place	Date	Hour	Summary of Events and Information	Remarks and references to Appendices
	June 5		Company Training was carried out on June 5 - 6	
	6			
	7		Battalion Training on June 7 - 8.	
	8		A considerable area of ground is available for the use of the Division, & within this area troops are permitted to move about our camps.	
	8		On the afternoon of June 8 the Brigade was inspected by the new Divisional Commander, Major General E.G.T. Bainbridge C.B.	
	9		Brigade training was carried out.	
	10			
	11		The Battalion had a Free Day - Church Parade was held in the morning, a Football match against 11/Lancashire Fusiliers was played in the afternoon & a concert was held in the evening.	
	12		Brigade training preparatory to Divisional Scheme on the following day.	
	13		Divisional Training.	

WAR DIARY or INTELLIGENCE SUMMARY

Army Form C. 2118

Place	Date	Hour	Summary of Events and Information	Remarks and references to Appendices
	14		The Battalion received orders to move from present area, & marched to MAIZIÈRES via BAILLEUL AUX CORNAILLES and AVERDOINGT.	6 miles
	15		One night was spent at MAIZIÈRES; the battalion moved on the following day to BARLY (about 15 miles) via ROUTE - SARS LES BOIS - RESBEUVIETTE - MONT LEBLOND - CANTELEUX.	15 miles
	16		The battalion remained at BARLY until the evening of the 17h when they marched to GÉZAINCOURT (near DOULLENS)	6 miles
	17			
	18		On the evening of the 18h the battalion again moved on to HALLOY - LES - PERNOIS.	9 miles
			In all the 4 days marching no man in the battalion fell out : a fact which is very creditable.	
	19 to 27		The Battalion remained at HALLOY - LES - PERNOIS : the time being spent in training.	

WAR DIARY
or
INTELLIGENCE SUMMARY
(Erase heading not required.)

Army Form C. 2118

Place	Date	Hour	Summary of Events and Information	Remarks and references to Appendices
E. of MONT ST. ELOY.	21		News was received that the following distinctions had been conferred on men of his battalion for gallantry on the night of May 21/22 during the assault by the Germans on BROADMARSH CRATER. DISTINGUISHED CONDUCT MEDAL No. 15522 Pte. JOHN. REGAN No. 15357 " JOHN SANGSTER MILITARY MEDAL No. 3565 Cpl. JOHN HENRY RICHARD HOROBIN COATES No. 20730 Pte. LEONARD ELKINS No. 15946 - ALBERT FINCH.	All of No 14 platoon and members of party under LT. JONES.

WAR DIARY
or
INTELLIGENCE SUMMARY
(Erase heading not required.)

Army Form C. 2118

Instructions regarding War Diaries and Intelligence Summaries are contained in F.S. Regs., Part II. and the Staff Manual respectively. Title Pages will be prepared in manuscript.

Place	Date	Hour	Summary of Events and Information	Remarks and references to Appendices
	27		The battalion received orders to march to HERISSART a distance of about 12 miles. The battalion marched at HALLOY-LES-PERNOIS at 10.15 pm & arrived at HERISSART at 2.45 am on the 28th.	12 miles
	28		Orders were received to march to LEALVILLERS a distance of about 5 miles, but were subsequently cancelled. The night of 28th was again spent at HERISSART.	
	29			
	30		The battalion remained at HERISSART until the evening of 30th when they marched to LEALVILLERS - a distance of about 5 miles - the night of the 30th was spent at ~~HERISSART~~ LEALVILLERS.	

G.B. Hennessy Lt. Col.
Comdg. 8/ Royal N. Lanc. R.

7th Bde.
25th Div.

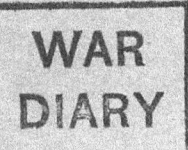

8th BATTALION

LOYAL NORTH LANCASHIRES.

JULY 1916.

8th. Royal N. Lanc. R
WAR DIARY VOLUME XI
or
INTELLIGENCE SUMMARY
July 1916.

Place	Date	Hour	Summary of Events and Information	Remarks and references to Appendices
LEALVILLERS	1st.		The day of June 1 was spent at LEALVILLERS: after 11 AM the Battalion was ordered to be ready to move at 1 hours notice. On June 1 the Franco - British Offensive North + South of the R. SOMME began. About 9.15 PM orders were received to move to FORCEVILLE about 4 miles to make room for the 38th Division - the Headwaters of which were coming to LEALVILLERS.	
	2nd.		The Battalion remained at FORCEVILLE until 10.45 pm on 2nd instant. When the whole Brigade moved into X Corps Reserve Area in AVELUY WOOD arriving there shortly before daybreak on 3rd. The 1st Line transport of the Battalion was separated from it + brigaded with the Brigade Transport Officer.	
	3rd.		The whole Brigade remained in AVELUY WOOD until the return of the 3rd. When the Brigade relieved the 14th Brigade in the trenches	

Army Form C. 2118

WAR DIARY or **INTELLIGENCE SUMMARY**
(Erase heading not required.)

Instructions regarding War Diaries and Intelligence Summaries are contained in F.S. Regs., Part II. and the Staff Manual respectively. Title Pages will be prepared in manuscript.

Place	Date	Hour	Summary of Events and Information	Remarks and references to Appendices
	3rd		This Battalion went into Brigade Reserve in dug outs at CRUCIFIX CORNER.	
	4th		The Battalion remained at CRUCIFIX CORNER during the 4th. The morning was spent in drawing up dug outs etc. The enemy shelled the area of CRUCIFIX CORNER considerably about 8.0 pm - the shells however did no damage. Our own artillery was also active again in the evening.	
	5th		There was a certain amount of hostile artillery activity about 3.30 pm and again at 5.30 pm. During the night of 5th/6th "C" Company was sent up to the trenches to work under orders of O.C. 3/Worcesters. An assault was made by the 4th/5th during the afternoon of the 5th in which they gained a further line of trenches in the LEIPZIG SALIENT. They had no less than 6 commanding officers. On the afternoon of 5th inst. the Chaplain attached to this Battalion (Rev. Father D. O'SULLIVAN) was killed by a	Ph.

Army Form C. 2118

WAR DIARY
or
INTELLIGENCE SUMMARY
(Erase heading not required.)

Instructions regarding War Diaries and Intelligence Summaries are contained in F.S. Regs., Part II. and the Staff Manual respectively. Title Pages will be prepared in manuscript.

Place	Date	Hour	Summary of Events and Information	Remarks and references to Appendices
		6h.	Shell outside the Advanced Dressing Station of 75th Field Ambulance. This is a loss which both O'Briens & men of the Battalion will feel deeply. The Battalion still remained at CRUCIFIX CORNER. Nothing of importance to record.	
		7h.	A heavy bombardment was carried out by our guns during the morning. At about 2 pm orders were received to move from CRUCIFIX CORNER up to the line. 2 companies (A & B) were sent up to the front line in accordance with orders, while Battalion Headquarters & D Company moved into trenches at CAMPBELL POST in the support line in front of AVELUY VILLAGE. C Company had already been sent into the line & placed at Disposal of O.C. 3rd WORCESTERS. These 3 companies (A, B & C) were subsequently moved up into the trenches of the LEIPZIG SALIENT which had been	

Army Form C. 2118

WAR DIARY
or
INTELLIGENCE SUMMARY
(Erase heading not required.)

Summary of Events and Information

captured from the Germans by the WILTSHIRE REGT. that morning.

At about 8.30 pm Battalion H/Q & D Coy moved up into the Salient & the Germans DB had position was taken over from the 3rd WORCESTER REGT. (1 company of WORCESTERS being kept to O.C. 87 L.N. Lanes for consistence)

The position was a difficult one especially in view of the fact that it had been taken over by night in absolute darkness. A German counter attack was expected but this did not actually take place. The night passed quietly except for desultory shelling & bombing. Our total casualties between 2 pm 7th & true of relief on early morning of 8th were as follows

OFFICERS: Killed 2 Lt. WHITE T.
Wounded 2 Lt WALSH P. (subsequently died of wounds)

OTHER RANKS: Killed 5
Wounded 34
missing: 2

Army Form C. 2118

WAR DIARY
or
INTELLIGENCE SUMMARY
(Erase heading not required.)

Place	Date	Hour	Summary of Events and Information	Remarks and references to Appendices
	8th		At about 6.0 AM the Battalion was relieved by 8th W. YORK. R. and moved to the casualty trenches in AVELUY WOOD where they remained until about midnight.	
	9th		At midnight 8th/9th the Battalion moved into bivouac near the ALBERT - POZIERES main road about 1 mile from ALBERT in support of the Brigade. The position was in support of 74th & 75th Brigades then in the newly won German line crossed OVILLERS and LA BOISSELLE. The morning & afternoon of 9th were spent in bivouac. At about 8.0 pm the Battalion moved up to the line with orders to take over part of the line held by 2nd ROYAL IRISH RIFLES and part of 11th LAN. FUS. of 74th Brigade. The line was an advanced line of trench system immediately south of OVILLERS.	

WAR DIARY or INTELLIGENCE SUMMARY

Army Form C. 2118

Place	Date	Hour	Summary of Events and Information	Remarks and references to Appendices
	10th		The relief was carried out successfully with only 2 casualties. The morning passed quietly. About 1.0 pm orders were received to occupy several points in the enemy line running across our front, points which this battalion was detailed to occupy were along the line 25.58, 51.73, 66.31, 93. (Ref. Sh. 57. D.S.E 1/5,000) At 2.30 pm an advance was made from our block at X.9.c.9.4. A heavy hostile barrage was opened on the French but in spite of very large casualties we reached point 25. Here we were held up by enemy bombing parties. Heavy shelling & bombing continued for about 2 hours without any gain. The enemy then tried to outflank us both on the left & right many crossing the open this counter attacks were however driven off. The night was quiet, a block being established just short of point 25. A detached post under Sgt. Holmes (C Coy) on the left of our line at X.8.d.9.9 held their ground all day although they had heavy casualties & no support could be	

got to them. They repulsed an enemy attack in force during the afternoon. Gun post was relieved during the night by 10h/11h by a party of B 10th Cheshires.

It is believed that the enemy was preparing a strong counter attack & that he took the initiative from him. Since he received plenty of reinforcements & appeared to be massing at various points notably at POZIERES WOOD which was observed by us & reported to Artillery. Concentrated artillery fire was opened on this area & heavy casualties were inflicted on the enemy since they were packed very close & our fire was accurate.

This battalion was later reinforced by 3D WORCESTER. R. but it is believed that when the attack was at its height & this battalion was standing alone, at least 3 German Prussian battalions were opposing it.

Desultory bombing & shell fire continued until the early hours of the morning of the 11th July.

Our casualties were very heavy in connection with this pushes as was only to be expected

CASUALTIES

OFFICERS KILLED. 2 LT DAY.
                "   "   PRINGLE.
                "   "   EMERSON.
                "   "   GRIMSHAW.

         WOUNDED. MAJOR WYNNE
                   CAPT. HADLEY
                   "   BENNETT
                   LT.   HOWARTH
                   "   SUMNER.

OTHER RANKS KILLED.   33
             WOUNDED. 156
             MISSING. 49 (believed killed)

Army Form C. 2118

WAR DIARY
or
INTELLIGENCE SUMMARY
(Erase heading not required.)

Place	Date	Hour	Summary of Events and Information	Remarks and references to Appendices
	11th		On the evening of 11th the Battalion was relieved in the front line & moved back into dug outs in LA BOISELLE	
	12th		Day passed quietly - nothing of importance to record.	
	13th		On the evening of 13th the Battalion received orders to move up in support of 10th Cheshire R. who were making an attack on OVILLERS. The attack however could not proceed owing to being held up by machine gun fire & was postponed until the following evening.	
	14th		At 11.30 pm 10th Cheshire R. made an attack on OVILLERS with orders to capture a line of trenches in S. part of village & then to push on to occupy the rest line at 2.0 AM in conjunction with 75th M.G. Brigade. This Battalion formed a carrying party & 11th Lancashire Fusiliers were in reserve. At 11.0 pm the attack was made & the enemys line was reached but had to be vacated owing to the machine gun fire from above.	[pm]

Army Form C. 2118

WAR DIARY
or
INTELLIGENCE SUMMARY
(Erase heading not required.)

Instructions regarding War Diaries and Intelligence Summaries are contained in F.S. Regs., Part II. and the Staff Manual respectively. Title Pages will be prepared in manuscript.

Place	Date	Hour	Summary of Events and Information	Remarks and references to Appendices
			Casualties for this operation were	
			Officers: Wounded: Capt. A.N. FALKNER (since died of wounds)	
			Lt. P.R. SHIELDS (slightly at duty)	
			O.R.: Killed: 3	
			Wounded: 11	
			Missing: 4	
	15th		On the afternoon of 15th the Brigade (less 3/WORCS. R.) was relieved by 74th Brigade & moved back in to bivouac near ALBERT.	
			On the evening of 15th OVILLERS was taken by 74th Brigade, the village surrendering with a garrison of 2 Officers & about 120 men.	
	16th		On evening of 16th the Battalion marched to FORCEVILLE & went in to billets.	
	17th		The Battalion remained at FORCEVILLE.	
	18th		On morning of 18th Battalion marched to BEAUVAL & went into billets.	

WAR DIARY
or
INTELLIGENCE SUMMARY
(Erase heading not required.)

Army Form C. 2118

Place	Date	Hour	Summary of Events and Information	Remarks and references to Appendices
	19th		The 19th was spent at BEAUVAL	
		20h	At 2.30 pm on 20h the Brigade moved from BEAUVAL & went into huts in BOIS DU WARNIMONT near AUTHIE.	
	21st 22nd		The battalion remained at BOIS DU WARNIMONT. Drafts of 60 & 90 men were received, many of these belonged to other units.	
	23rd		The 7th Brigade relieved the 86th Brigade (29th Divn) in the trenches N of River ANCRE. The 1st WILTS & 10th CHESHIRES relieved the 2 battalion in the line while 1st battalion & 3rd WORCESTERS went into reserve at ENGLEBELMER & MAILLY WOOD respectively.	
	24th		Battalion remained at ENGLEBELMER. Nothing of note to report.	

Army Form C. 2118

WAR DIARY
or
INTELLIGENCE SUMMARY
(Erase heading not required.)

Place	Date	Hour	Summary of Events and Information	Remarks and references to Appendices
	25th to 28th		The Battalion remained at ENGLEBELMER. This was spent in training new drafts. Drafts were received of 138 other ranks on 26th inst and 214 other ranks on 29th inst. Formed drafts chiefly composed of E. Lancs - Border - Manchesters - Kings	
	29th		The Battalion relieved 1st Wiltshire R. in trenches. Relief carried out successfully	

A.B. Stewart Lt. Col.
Cmdg. 8/N. Lan. R.

Reserve Army
G.A. 31/4/1.

25th Division G. 22/88

RESERVE ARMY SPECIAL ORDER.

The Commander of the Reserve Army wishes to express to the 25th and 32nd Divisions his high appreciation of the excellent work which they have done while under his command. They have been engaged day and night against a brave and determined enemy, who has had every advantage of ground, and by their perserverance and endurance they have done much to facilitate the task of the troops on their right. Progress has been steady, and the results achieved have been of great value to our cause. These Divisions are about to rest and refit and the Army Commander trusts that they will soon be ready to resume active operations.

Hd. Qrs.,　　　　　　　Sgd.　N. MALCOLM, Major General,
Reserve Army,　　　　　　　　　　　　　　General Staff.
16th July, 1916.

2.

7th Infantry Bde.
74th Infantry Bde.
75th Infantry Bde.
C.R.A., 25th Div.
C.R.E., 25th Div.
O.C., 6th Bn. S. B.
O.C., 25th Div. Sig. Co.
O.C., 25th Div. Train
A.D.M.S.
A.A.& Q.M.G.

1.　Forwarded for your information and communication to all troops under your command.

　　　　　　　　　　　　　　　　　　　　　　Major,
　　　　　　　　　　　　　　　　　　　General Staff,
17/7/16.　　　　　　　　　　　　　　　　　25th Division.

SPECIAL ORDER OF THE DAY

BY

Lieut-General Sir T.L.N.MORLAND, K.C.B., D.S.O.

17th July 1916

============:oO)(Oo:============

On their withdrawal from the line after 11 days hard fighting the G.O.C. wishes to express to the G.O.C. and all ranks of the 25th Division his appreciation of their gallantry and devotion to duty and congratulates them on the final success of their efforts in OVILLERS.

------oO)(Oo------

(Sd) G.WEBB. Brigadier-General.
D.A. & Q.M.G.,
X Corps.

SPECIAL ORDER OF THE DAY

BY

Brig. General C.E.HEATHCOTE, D.S.O., Commanding

7th Infantry Brigade.

The B.G.C. would like to congratulate the units of the 7th Brigade on their splendid record of the last fortnight.

All ranks have shewn their gallant behaviour in the face of the enemy that they can add fresh laurels to the glorious records of their Regiments and increase the high reputation of the Brigade whenever the opportunity occurs.

When all have done so well, it would be invidious to mention special Regiments but the B.G.C. feels that the good work of the 7th Brigade Machine Gun Company under Captain J.A.RUTHERFORD and the 7th Trench Mortar Battery under Lieut A.HARRISON should be recorded here.

The work of these valuable and quite indispensible units of the Brigade is apt to be overlooked or at any rate to get out of perspective when compared with the work of the larger units, but the B.G.C. feels certain that all ranks of the battalions fully realise how devotedly and efficiently they have been supported by the machine and Stokes guns.

The B.G.C. deeply deplores the loss of so many fallen Officers, N.C.O's and men but the Brigade well knows that these lives have not been given in vain. No effort will be spared to live up to and increase the reputation bequeathed to each unit by those who have laid down their lives in the fore front of the battle.

While urging them to fresh efforts in training and preparation, the B.G.C. feels sure that it must be source of great satisfaction to ALL ranks to feel that the arduous days of last month have borne good fruit.

The lessons of each phrase of the fighting must however be considered and made full use of and there must be no pause in tthe careful and methodical preparation for the final victory.

Finally it must be satisfactory to all ranks to know that the Division (of which the 7th Brigade forms such an important part) has made a great reputation for itself in this first phrase of the advance and the B.G.C. has no hesitation in saying that this reputation is due in no small measure to the part played by every individual under his command.

---oO)(Oo---

* 8/h Loyal N. Lanc R.
attached 7/h T.M Battery

EXTRACT FROM
ROUTINE ORDERS BY
MAJOR-GENERAL E.G.T. BAINBRIDGE C.B.
COMMANDING 25th DIVISION.

HEADQUARTERS
17 JULY 1916.

MESSAGE FROM ARMY COMMANDER.

1247.   Xth Corps wire begins:

"Please convey to the 25th Division the Army Commander's thanks for their splendid work in OVILLERS."

(Signed)
R. F. LEGGE.
LT. COL.
A.A. & Q.M.G. 25th Division

7th Brigade.
25th Division.

1/8th BATTALION

LOYAL NORTH LANCASHIRE REGIMENT

AUGUST 1 9 1 6

Appendices attached :- Patrol Reports.

WAR DIARY

Army Form C. 2118

WAR DIARY
—or—
INTELLIGENCE SUMMARY
(Erase heading not required.)

Army Form C. 2118

Place	Date	Hour	Summary of Events and Information	Remarks and references to Appendices
	July 30		No occurrence of note – Enemy generally fairly quiet during day. At night he uses his French mortars and guns against new front line on which we are working about 300 x in advance of our old front line on the night of 31/7. Capt B.W. FISH and Sergt H. HOLMES made a very good reconnaissance starting out from our Right Coy at 10.30 pm. The Patrol remained out altogether until 1.50 am making 3 separate journeys. The ground between various posts held by us was thoroughly reconnoitred, notably between LANCASHIRE POST and CROWS NEST POST & between PICTURE DROME POST and the enemys first line & wire. Division expressed himself very pleased with the G.O.C. which this patrol was carried out.	
	31			

WAR DIARY
INTELLIGENCE SUMMARY

Army Form C. 2118

31 AUG 1916

Instructions regarding War Diaries and Intelligence Summaries are contained in F.S. Regs, Part II. and the Staff Manual respectively. Title Pages will be prepared in manuscript.

(Erase heading not required.)

Place	Date	Hour	Summary of Events and Information	Remarks and references to Appendices
	August 1		On the night of Aug 1/2 an attempt was made to establish an advanced post on our line & running towards German line. This was done as the result of Capt FISH's reconnaissance of previous night: every attempt at it made to occupy the position was however observed by the enemy, who, it is thought must have seen Capt FISH's patrol; heavy fire was opened & the point could not be gained.	
	2		A subsequent attempt was made on the evening of 2/3 but as soon as our patrol went out it was discovered that the enemy already had a post out at this place. The post withdrew on the approach of our men and just before our party arrived at point where post was to be established the enemy put 3 "minenwerfer" bombs into the position. But it was eventually that the Johnstely he barrage was gone. On our returning...	

1875 Wt. W593/826 1,000,000 4/15 J.B.C. & A. A.D.S.S./Forms/C. 2118.

WAR DIARY
or
INTELLIGENCE SUMMARY

(Erase heading not required.)

Place	Date	Hour	Summary of Events and Information	Remarks and references to Appendices
	Aug 3 4 5		The Battalion remained in the trenches; nothing of importance to record. A new fire & support trench is being dug in advance of our old front line. There have been an often heavy shelled both by enemy's guns & also trench mortars when our men are working on them during the hours of darkness.	
	6		The Battalion was relieved by the 2nd D.L.I. the 50th Division being relieved by the 6th Division. Battalion went in to Divisional Reserve at BERTRANCOURT.	
	7 8 9 10		The Battalion remained at BERTRANCOURT & carried on the training of new Drafts. The Battalion moved on to VAUCHELLES, where training was continued.	

WAR DIARY
or
INTELLIGENCE SUMMARY

(Erase heading not required.)

Army Form C. 2118

Instructions regarding War Diaries and Intelligence Summaries are contained in F.S. Regs., Part II. and the Staff Manual respectively. Title Pages will be prepared in manuscript.

Place	Date	Hour	Summary of Events and Information	Remarks and references to Appendices
	11 to 14		Training of the draft was carried on. 6 hand work a day being done.	
	15		The battalion moved from VAUCHELLES to PUCHEVILLERS. The whole Brigade attacked units being billeted in this village.	
	17		The whole Brigade marched from PUCHEVILLERS to HEDAUVILLE bivouacked in grounds of the Chateau.	
	18		On the morning of 18th the 3 other Battalions of his Brigade went into the trenches whilst his battalion remained in Brigade Reserve & HEDAUVILLE & carried on training.	
	19/22		During this period the Bath carried on training at HEDAUVILLE.	
	23		The Batt. marched from HEDAUVILLE to Dugouts in the South BLUFF at BLACK HORSE BR & 66 close to AVELUY WOOD, arriving there in support of troops in the LEIPZIG SALIENT. "A" Coy went into dugouts at Lock Pit	

1875. Wt. W593/826 1,000,000 4/15 J.B.C. & A. A.D.S.S./Forms/C. 2118.

WAR DIARY
or
INTELLIGENCE SUMMARY

(Erase heading not required.)

Army Form C. 2118

Place	Date	Hour	Summary of Events and Information	Remarks and references to Appendices
	Aug. 24th		At 2 p.m. "A" & "B" Coys. these batts. went into the LEIPZIG SALIENT to act in support to the 1/WILTSHIRE REGT. while "C" Coy was attached to the 3rd WORCESTERSHIRE REGT. These two Batts. were to take the HINDENBERG Trench. At 4 p.m. whilst this was successfully done, the enemy turned on a very heavy artillery barrage and "A" & "B" Coys. suffered many casualties during the supplementary. "C" Coy. acted as a carrying party, No. 3 Pn. remained at the BLUFF.	
	25th		"A" & "B" Coys. took over the captured trench from the 1/WILTSHIRE REGT. and the bombers fought during most of the day. In the evening orders were received that the Batt. should relieve the 1/WILTS. REGT. next morning and take over the trenches the 1/WILTS. REGT. had failed to take.	
	26th		At 6 a.m. "C", "D" and "D" Coys. moved up into the SALIENT. "C" Coy. moving up by daylight, and the whole time were under fire. Preparations were made for the capture of the trench allotted to the Batt. Information received during the day that this trench was to be held by no less than 100 Germans who have been strongly and ready to surrender. "B" Coy. and "C" Coy. attacked the trench. At 6 p.m. the trench was stormed & captured by our finest bombing, live resistance the trench being very heavy then and Lieut. MARTIN from whose fire and M.G. fire the loss arose. & seconds his following the first happened very heavily indeed. Our artillery helped us.	

WAR DIARY or INTELLIGENCE SUMMARY

Army Form C. 2118

31 AUG 1916 — (Ser) Bn. Loyal North Lancs

The survivors of "A" Coy were entered. The Germans turned & fired at very close range led by very determined men. 2 fierce fights ensued, the being heavily outnumbered, Lieut. COPEMAN being that the fight was hopeless, he no lost across "A" Coy, "B" Coy, leaving Lieut. SHIELDS with 30 men of "B" Coy, to cover the new trenches which were being heavily shelled all the time. he been holding positions in the enemy's third & then Lieut. COPEMAN was last a very strong German Counter attack was being made & passed for no Trenches. Lightly held by Lieut. SHIELDS and his few men, this Can having up a very stout resistance. Lieut. COPEMAN at once saw the idea of taking his German trench & went to keep them no to leave it for Capture. & an attacking forces from being cut off, the boys shielded & withdrew all of our men save 1 who been left and left them here to hand back. SHIELDS. The enemy attacked in great strength several Times but by them officers & infficient boys being brave on his and finally beat his off. Lieut. G.E. CASH the Commanded the attack, Lieut. MAY and Lieut. PIGOTT were lost from the German third & is believes that all have been Killed. Henry shelling continued to some hours and when attempts round the rest of the night. Our artillery afforded no truth Protection to them Counterfor Our losses in this engagement, Killed, wounded and missing killed Robards 4 officers and 85 other ranks. 3 officers and 181 other ranks.

WAR DIARY
or
INTELLIGENCE SUMMARY

Army Form C. 2118

Place	Date	Hour	Summary of Events and Information	Remarks and references to Appendices
	27th		The Bn. marched to Bn. of S. Lancs. Regt. at mining and moved to Hedauville, and billeted, arriving there about 3 P.M.	
	28th		The Brigade was inspected and congratulated for its fine work by Lieut. Genl. Jacob, Cmdg. II Corps. After the inspection the Battn. marched to Bouzincourt into billets.	
	29th		Battn. carried on training at BOUZINCOURT.	
	30th		Owing to bad weather work was carried out in billets at BOUZINCOURT. The following was received at 11 A.M. from Corps Commander, II Corps. "The Corps Commander has read the report of the minor operation carried out on the afternoon of the 26th inst. by the 8th Battn. The Loyal N. Lancashire Regt. The attack although unsuccessful was carried out most gallantly. The arrangement made by the Battn. Commander were good, & it was due to no fault of his or his men that the operation failed. While regretting the heavy casualties the Corps Commander congratulates Lieut. Col. MARRIOTT and all ranks of the 8th Battn. the Loyal N. Lancashire Regt. on the spirit and gallantry with which the attack was	

WAR DIARY
INTELLIGENCE SUMMARY

Army Form C. 2118

Place	Date	Hour	Summary of Events and Information	Remarks and references to Appendices
	31/8	9	made. The men fought splendidly & their work was worthy of high praise. The following was received at the same time from G.O.C. 25th Divn. "The Divisional Commander thoroughly agrees with the remarks of the Corps Commander. Please communicate to O.C. 8th Bath the LOYAL N. LANCASHIRE Rgt." The Bath was supplying two and working parties to work just behind the line at OVILLERS and at AVELUY. During the evening the GERMANS dropped about a dozen shells of fairly small calibre into BOUZINCOURT. No one in this Battn was injured.	

WAR DIARY
INTELLIGENCE SUMMARY

Place	Date	Hour	Summary of Events and Information	Remarks and references to Appendices
	August 1-31		During the month of August 1916, the following honours & rewards were published and awarded. LIEUT. R.B.B. JONES. 8th Bn. LOYL. N. LANCS. Rgt. received the VICTORIA CROSS "for most conspicuous bravery. He was holding with his platoon a crater recently captured from the enemy. About 7.30pm the enemy exploded a mine forty yards to his right, and at the same time put a heavy barrage of fire on our trenches, thus isolating the platoon. Lieut. Jones kept attacked in overwhelming numbers. Lieut. JONES kept his men together, steadying them by his fine example, and shot no fewer than fifteen of the enemy as they advanced, counting them aloud so as to cheer his men. When his ammunition was expended, he took a bomb, but was shot through the head when he was getting up to throw it. His splendid courage had so encouraged his men that when they had no more ammunition & bombs left, they threw stones and ammunition boxes at the enemy till only nine of the platoon were left. Finally, they were compelled to retire." Date 9/16 Gallant act was May 21st 1916.	

WAR DIARY
INTELLIGENCE SUMMARY
(Erase heading not required.)

Summary of Events and Information

The following officers received the D.S.O.
MAJOR. F.G. WYNNE. 8/N. LAN. R.   10/7/16
CAPT. S. RAMSAY.   8/N. LAN. R.   10/7/16
CAPT. A. HARRISON. 8/N. LAN. R. (cmdg. 7th T.M. Batty) 10/7/16

The following officer received the MILITARY CROSS (see report of July 31st)
CAPT. B.W. FISH. 8/N. LAN. R.

The following N.C.O. and men have been decorated.
No. 15779 SERGT. H. HOLMES. MILITARY MEDAL. 30.7/16
No. 13640 SERGT. T. SEED.   MILITARY MEDAL.   3.8.16
No. 15253 PTE. NUTTALL.   D.C.M.   10/7/16

P.B. Kennett
LIEUT. COLONEL
COMMANDING 8th LOYAL NORTH LANC. 2nd... REGT.

REPORT OF PATROLS DURING NIGHT of JULY 31st - AUGUST
1st   1916.

Map Reference.
BEAUMONT   57.d.S.E.

      The first patrol went out at 10.30 p.m. from CORNER POST along the row of trees towards the EAST of the pond shewn on Map at Q.24.a. and Q.18.c.   This "pond" is of the nature of a marsh at present.

      The trench shewn E of "pond" on Map is wet and the first few yards shewed no signs of occupation.

      At Q.18.c.70 there is an enemy post which was then held by four or five men.   The post was protected by weak wire stretched from tree to tree and round brushwood towards S.

      On the N. and E sides of the trench the wire is <u>very strong</u> consisting of barbed wire on stakes, round brushwood etc etc.

      The ground on the East of the pond to the river, is now, after days of dry weather, impassable.   There is some wire but it is weak.   The whole is marshy and in many places waist deep.

      There is no possible position to the East of a line running from the "pond" to the MILL for a "post"

      The patrol could find no signs of the enemy having done any patrolling on the ground East of the pond to the river.

      A machine gun was firing at the MILL from some point about Q.18.d.80 and one of the heavy trench mortars was firing towards the new support trench from somewhere in Q.24.b.42

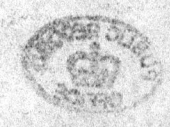

The patrol came in and went out again from LANCASHIRE POST along the hedge at the top of the Railway embankment northwards towards the enemy block at Q.18.c.53

An excellent place for a post was found on the embankment about 60 yards from the enemy's block

This could be constructed out of view of the enemy; there is a very good communication to it and from it a good view over the enemy's trench on E side of the "pond" can be obtained.

If necessary an advanced listening post could be formed in front of this position that would be within 30 yards of the enemy's block.

From the suggested post the ground slopes gradually down to the enemy's position, in front of which the wire is very strong indeed,

Work was going on here, rails were being handled and it is thought that blasting was going on in the West side of the Railway Embankment.

There is a dugout or sap in this embankment and a machine gun emplacement seem in course of construction.

The patrol afterwards went out from the PICTUREDROME Post and went along the Western Embankment as far as the enemy wire. This is low trip wire about 1 foot high and weak.

A night listening post could well be placed here.

The patrol stayed a considerable time here and heard men working and drilling metal.

No idea of the strength of the garrison could be found, several men were heard.

It is the opinion of the patrol that, the wire East

of the Embankment and South of the trench having been destroyed a minor enterprise conducted simultaneously along both sides of the Railway might succeed in occupying the enemy's position but that this <u>could not be held</u> as it is enfiladed from high ground on both flanks. (rough sketch attached.

sd B.W.FISH, Capt,
5th L.N.Lancs.
1/8/16.

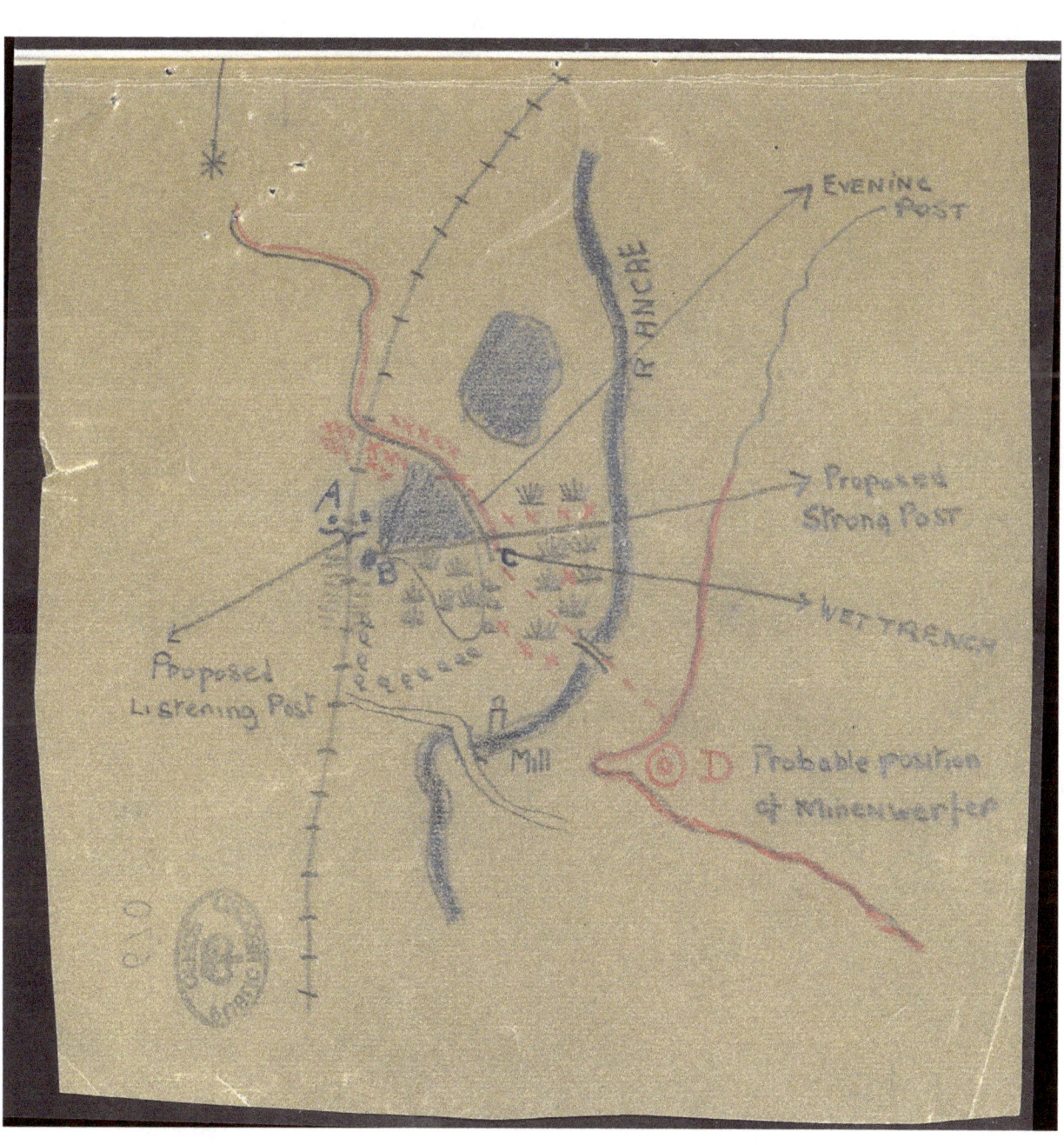

7th. INFANTRY BDE.

25th. DIVISION

8th. LOYAL NORTH LANCS. REGT.

SEPTEMBER 1916.

WAR DIARY
INTELLIGENCE SUMMARY

(Erase heading not required.)

Army Form C. 2118

7/75
8 LN Fusiliers
Vol 12

Place	Date	Hour	Summary of Events and Information	Remarks and references to Appendices
BOUZINCOURT	Sept 1916 1st		The Batn was still in the same billets. Small fatigue parties were supplied to work at OVILLERS-LA-BOISELLE and at BOUZINCOURT for recovery of the Bath carried on training, and also had hot baths	
	2nd – 4th		The Batn remained at BOUZINCOURT, finding working parties and carried on training.	
	5th		The Batn marched from BOUZINCOURT to LEALVILLERS, where it was accommodated in billets.	
	6th		The Batn. was at LEALVILLERS and occupied the day in training.	
	7th		The Batn left LEALVILLERS at 9am and marched to RAINCHEVAL, a distance of 3½ miles, where it was accommodated in billets. During the afternoon the training was carried out.	
	Strength		Batn moved RAINCHEVAL carrying out training	
	10th		Batn moved to LONGUEVILLETTE, where it was billeted.	
	11th		Batn moved to PROUVILLE, a distance of about 10 miles, where it was billeted.	Fr

WAR DIARY
or
INTELLIGENCE SUMMARY

Army Form C. 2118

Place	Date	Hour	Summary of Events and Information	Remarks and references to Appendices
	12th		The Batt. moved to COULONVILLIERS, a distance of about 6 miles, where they were billeted. A new draft of 300 men from the MANCHESTER R. arrived & was attached to the Batt.	
	13th-24th		The Batt. was at COULONVILLIERS carrying out training. Batt. sports were held on the 23rd at 2 p.m.	
	25th		The Batt. marched to LONGUEVILLETTE, a distance of about 13 miles, where they were billeted.	
	26th		The Batt. marched to RAINCHEVAL, a distance of about 9 miles, where they were billeted.	
	27th / 28th		The Battalion at RAINCHEVAL carried out training, in trenches digging etc. and night operations.	

Army Form C. 2118

WAR DIARY
or
INTELLIGENCE SUMMARY
(Erase heading not required.)

Place	Date	Hour	Summary of Events and Information	Remarks and references to Appendices
	29th		The Battalion moved to HEDAUVILLE (a distance of about 7 miles) to Billets where they rested overnight.	
	30th		The Battalion moved into the trenches, where they relieved the LINCOLNSHIRE R. in the sector HESSIAN TRENCH, west of STUFF REDOUBT.	
			Honors & awards were allotted to this Battⁿ during the month of September 1916 — as under	
			Lieut Hugh Douglas COPEMAN } Military Cross	
			Lieut Peter Robo SHIELDS }	
			N° 015243 Pte Thomas NUTTALL D.C.M. — awarded Russian Order "Cross St George 4th Class"	
			N° 014320 C.S.M. Walter POWELL }	
			" 4235 Sgt Hugh HORROCKS } D.C.M.	
			" 15464 Sgt James A. TINSLEY }	
			" 12650 Cpl Harvey FEARNEHOUGH }	
			" 15074 Pte John MANN }	
			" 16207 Pte James MATHER } Military Medal	
			" 13738 Pte Thomas McGARR }	

A. V. Hinnworth Lieut Col
Comdg 8th (S) Battⁿ Royal North Lancashire Reg^t

7th INFANTRY BDE.

25th DIVISION.

8th BATTALION.

LOYAL NORTH LANCASHIRE REGIMENT.

OCTOBER 1916

Vol 13
Army Form C. 2118

8th Bn Loyal N Lancs Regt

WAR DIARY
INTELLIGENCE SUMMARY
(Erase heading not required.)

Place	Date	Hour	Summary of Events and Information	Remarks and references to Appendices
B.E.F.	1/10/16		The Battn was in the left sector of the Brigade front, in HESSIAN TRENCH. S.W. of STUFF REDOUBT.	
	3/10/16		The Battn was relieved in the evening by the 3rd WORCESTER. R, and proceeded to the reserve line dugouts, which were in the original GERMAN front line at X.2.a (1250 yds. N. of OVILLERS).	
	4th to 8th		Battn were in reserve line supplying working & carrying parties for troops in the forward area.	
	9th		The Battn relieved the Xth Cheshire R. in the STUFF REDOUBT area.	
	9th		The Battn was relieved by the Xth Cheshire R. in the STUFF REDOUBT area during the morning. The Battn then returned to the reserve line N. of OVILLERS.	
	10th		The Battn relieved the Xth Cheshire Regt in the STUFF REDOUBT area at 2pm. The Battn now occupied the Northern face of STUFF REDOUBT which was captured by the X Cheshire R. on the previous evening.	
	11th		The usual trench warfare was carried on & the enemy made two very feeble attempts to enter our line at a bombing post N.? point 18, but met with no success in either case.	

WAR DIARY

INTELLIGENCE SUMMARY

(Erase heading not required.)

Army Form C. 2118

Place	Date	Hour	Summary of Events and Information	Remarks and references to Appendices
B.E.F.	19/10/16		At 6.45 p.m. the enemy made a very determined attack on STUFF REDOUBT. He assaulted at 3 points viz. about bombing post N.7 points 18, and 38, & about the barricade across STUMP ROAD. The enemy appeared with great cunning & was not discovered until a shower of bombs was hurled on to our post. About 30 of the enemy advanced against each of our positions. The attempt on point 38 and on the STUMP RD. barricade were easily beaten off, but at point 18, on the left, he effected an entry into our line & bombed his way down to C.T. as far as point 118. Our artillery barrage was most effective, & prevented these supports being brought up. The enemy bombed our 76m. trench dugouts, and used our own bomb dump against us. At point 18 he was checked, and a very fierce fight ensued here for more than 30 minutes, before we succeeded in expelling the enemy from our position. The GERMANS established touch dump the 76m as ten points in our trench when he had penetrated. When the enemy found that his attempts were not coming up, he retired from our trench. Those who escaped being killed by our Lewis Guns were certainly caught in the Barrage. At 9.20 p.m. the enemy made a counter attack which although attacked the vigour of the first attack	

Army Form C. 2118

WAR DIARY
INTELLIGENCE SUMMARY
(Erase heading not required.)

Place	Date	Hour	Summary of Events and Information	Remarks and references to Appendices
B.E.F.	12.10.16		Called for Stan. The enemy raiding parties were one of the professional touring parties known as "STORM TROOPS". From information received later, the casualties w/h were two "STORM TROOP" were very heavy. Our casualties were Capt. E.S. UNDERHILL, killed; and 3 other Capt. Chatsworth Musgrave & Lieut. Golden (R.A.M.C.) wounded. Capt. P.S. Other ranks killed 9 wounded.	
	13.10.16		The day was spent clearing up the trenches & reorganising the front dumps prior to an attack which was being made on the Reserve.	
	14.10.16		At 2.46 p.m. an attack was made by B Co. under Capt. R.R. SHIELDS against two enemy trenches running in a N.W. direction from the N. face of STUFF REDOUBT to STUFF TRENCH. The objective was to gain a footing on the crest of the hill so as to obtain observation of the enemy in the valley beyond. At 2.54 p.m. the objective had been secured, and every shift was to our troops. The position was at once put in a temporary state of defence, while the permanent	

WAR DIARY or INTELLIGENCE SUMMARY

Army Form C. 2118

Place	Date	Hour	Summary of Events and Information	Remarks and references to Appendices
B.E.F	14.10.16		consolidation was carried out with great skill & determination. One Officer and 110 other ranks were taken prisoner & sent to the rear. In the L/T C.T. the enemy offered a small resistance by throwing bombs into the trench from the bottom [dugout]. This obstacle was however overcome, & the enemy either killed or captured. 20 Germans were found dead in it, & another 35 who put up a fight in the trench were either bayoneted or shot. One machine gun, one bomb thrower and some telephone equipment, as well as arms & equipment etc were captured. For this attack 114 men + 3 Officers were employed. These figures include carrying & mopping up parties. The enemy was caught astride an unfortunate moment for himself, a relief had just been completed, & the new troops were not properly settled in. The operation was in every respect successful in every respect; all frontal required trenches captured & consolidated. Our casualties in the actual taking of the position were 1 Officer wounded, 8 Other ranks killed and 120 Other ranks wounded. 17.39 total	

WAR DIARY
INTELLIGENCE SUMMARY

(Erase heading not required.)

Army Form C. 2118

Place	Date	Hour	Summary of Events and Information	Remarks and references to Appendices
	15.10.16		The Battⁿ was relieved at 9am by the 2/South Lancs. R. After relief the Battⁿ marched to a camp close to BOUZINCOURT where it was accommodated in tents.	SOUTH LANCS R. RESERVE BOUZINCOURT
	16.10.16		The following was received from the Army Commander. "Please convey the congratulations of the Army Commander to the 25th Divn on the excellent arrangements made and the splendid work & gallantry displayed by the troops in the operations carried out in the neighbourhood of STUFF REDOUBT during the last few days." The following was received from B.G.C. 7th Corps Bde. "The B.G.C. wishes the Army Commander's message to be circulated to all ranks, and himself wishes to congratulate the whole Brigade on the splendid work in the trenches during the past fortnight."	RESERVE ARMY STUFF REDOUBT 7th Corps Bde.
	17.10.16		"A" & "C" Coys were sent up to the support line to relieve carrying parties for the 75th Inf. Bde. in view of forthcoming operations. The remainder of the Battⁿ remained near BOUZINCOURT.	75th Inf. Bde. BOUZINCOURT

Army Form C. 2118

WAR DIARY
INTELLIGENCE SUMMARY
(Erase heading not required.)

Instructions regarding War Diaries and Intelligence Summaries are contained in F.S. Regs., Part II. and the Staff Manual respectively. Title Pages will be prepared in manuscript.

Place	Date	Hour	Summary of Events and Information	Remarks and references to Appendices
	19.10.16		'A' 'C' Coy returned to camp in BOUZINCOURT during the morning. During very bad weather conditions, very little training was carried out. During the afternoon, GEN. SIR. H. de la P. GOUGH, KCB. cmdg the Reserve Army, visited the Battn & congratulated on its recent success.	
	20.		The Battn carried out training in the morning. In the afternoon a football match was played between A'+'B' Coys versus C'+'D' Coys. The Battn moved into billets in the village of sub BOUZINCOURT at	
	21.		9 AM. The Battn marched to RUBEMPRÉ where it was billeted.	
	22.		The Battn marched to LONGUEVILLETTE where it was billeted.	
	23.		The Battn carried out training at LONGUEVILLETTE.	
	24-28		The Battn left by train from DOULLENS at 11.50pm to travel to BAILLEUL in the Second Army area. The Battn arrived at BAILLEUL at 8am & then marched to PONT DE NIEPPE near	
	29		ARMENTIÈRES, where they were billeted. A+B Coys were billeted close to the church in NIEPPE, & the remainder of the Battn close to PONT. DE. NIEPPE.	

WAR DIARY
or
INTELLIGENCE SUMMARY

(Erase heading not required.)

Army Form C. 2118

Place	Date	Hour	Summary of Events and Information	Remarks and references to Appendices
	30.10.16		The Battn. arrived in billets at PONT DE NIEPPE.	
	"		The C.O. & Coy Cmdrs went round the line preparatory to taking over on Nov 1st/16.	
			The following awards have been received during the month.—	
			Capt. P.R. SHIELDS. Bar to Military Cross.	
			2/Lieut. E.R. ALFORD " Military Cross	
			" P.L. BOLTON. Military Cross	
			" E. TURNER. Military Cross	
			12650 Sgt. H. FERRINGHOUGH. Bar to D.C.M.	
			16895 " G. HUTCHINSON. D.C.M	
			4285 " W. PASQUILL. D.C.M	
			8215 Pte. HUMPHRIES. D.C.M.	
			24521 Pte. KILLALLON. D.C.M	
			12762 Pte. SPEAKMAN D.C.M.	
			15126 Sgt. BARNES. M.M.	
			15464 " TINSLEY. M.M.	
			15790 Pte. CARTWRIGHT. M.M.	
			17999 Pte. LEATHER. M.M.	
			27076 Pte. ELLISON. M.M	
			13591 L/cpl. BOARDMAN. M.M	
			12213 Pte. BURTON. M.M.	
			17604 Sgt. CROSBY. M.M.	
			13606 Pte. POLLITT. M.M.	
			6822 Pte WORDSWORTH. M.M.	
			10451 Pte SCHOFIELD. M.M.	

N.J. Maxwell Major.
Cmdg. 8th Loyal. N. Lancs. R.

7th INFANTRY BDE
25th DIVISION.

8th BATTALION,

LOYAL NORTH LANCASHIRE REGIMENT.

NOVEMBER 1916

692

Army Form C. 2118

WAR DIARY
INTELLIGENCE SUMMARY
(Erase heading not required.)

8th Loyal North Lanc Regt

Place	Date	Hour	Summary of Events and Information	Remarks and references to Appendices
In the field	1.11.16		The Battn relieved the 2nd Bn Ye Gordon Highlanders in the Brigade support line of the LE TOUQUET sector. A & C Coys 8/N. Lan. R. were taking over the supporting points on GUNNERS FM — STATION REDOUBT — LYS FM line, and B & D Coys were in the N. end of LE BIZET.	
	2.11.16 to 6.11.16 inclus		The Battn was in support as detailed above, employed chiefly in building up the defences, and reconnoitring the front line.	
	7.11.16		The Battn relieved the 3rd Bn Worcestershire Regt in Right Sub-sector of the Brigade front line. This is from Essex Farm Central to the Cromer Beer — the nearest point of line to River Lys. Also Craig — an isolated post midway between Lens of Line and River also held by small garrison. Patrols from Lys Farm visit Aston Craig by night and from line to Aston Craig. The sector of line held includes LE TOUQUET SALIENT. The left Coy is about 50 yds distant from the enemy — thence to right the line recedes from each other until the right Coy is nearer to the enemy on the other side of the river than the enemy are on our own side of the river.	Pn

Army Form C. 2118

WAR DIARY
INTELLIGENCE SUMMARY
(Erase heading not required.)

Instructions regarding War Diaries and Intelligence Summaries are contained in F. S. Regs, Part II. and the Staff Manual respectively. Title Pages will be prepared in manuscript.

Place	Date	Hour	Summary of Events and Information	Remarks and references to Appendices
	7-11-16		The trenches are in a very bad state. Little work seems to have been done on them during the summer. The wet weather is flooding the swampy land near the river and the trenches are acting as drains to the land around. Ditches seem to be blocked so trenches do not drain. Much manage work required and also work on communication trenches. Engaged on our right across Rivr. Lys.	
	7-11-16 to 13-11-16		Engaged on draining, pumping, and revetting work. Heavy rain came. Many falls of cadre of trenches. Enemy active with heavy trench mortars. We retaliated by Stokes Mortars and Artillery tried many aeroplane grenades. Also horizons two silence enemy "minnie". Not many casualties. Became lively later and many Safos. - See sketch map. Two Lewis and Machine Guns Guard trees. Two discharged by us from our front along with fatte artillery bombardment. No retaliation from enemy. Battalion relieved by 3rd Worcesters and went into Bde Reserve at	
	11-11-16 to 13-11-16		PONT DE NIEPPE. Three companies in wooden huts and one in brick buildings — probably an old brewery.	
	13-11-16 to 15-11-16		Battalion had baths and was fitted with new tos respirators. Daily fatigue party to keep village clean. Another two ready for work in R.E. dumps. After these, every available man went daily for working parties on manage work and revetting of trenches — chiefly communication	

WAR DIARY
or
INTELLIGENCE SUMMARY

(Erase heading not required.)

Army Form C. 2118

Place	Date	Hour	Summary of Events and Information	Remarks and references to Appendices
	19-11-16		Trenches in both right and left sub-sectors. We relieved 3rd Worcesters in front line trenches. Much work done on trenches — drainage work beginning to show effect, but water still high. River rising: Aisow being abandoned but TOOL HOUSE garrisons invested. Supply of hot soup at night and newly changing wet socks and gumboots kept men's feet in good order. The cases of sickness & trench feet is very low, shows we have enemy again active with heavy "minnies", also many men, shows we have no effective means of retaliation by mortars — rely on artillery.	
	25-11-16		Battn. relieved and moved into Supporting Park holding Hyp Farm, Stirling Redoubt, Seven Tree Redoubt, Rescue Farm, Paternoster Row, Fort Paul, and Lancashire Support Trench with a Coy, and a half Coy in LE BIZET.	
	25-11-16 to 30-11-16		Much work done on redoubts — rebuilding traps, revetting & draining.	
	1-12-16		Relieved 3rd Worcesters in front line. Awards announced during month for work on Somme —	

Lt. Col. G. B. MARRIOTT   D.S.O.
A/Capt P.R. SHIELDS   Bar to M.C.
Lieut J.S. HILL   M.C.
2/Lieut P.L. BOLTON   M.C.

WAR DIARY
or
INTELLIGENCE SUMMARY

(Erase heading not required.)

Army Form C. 2118

Place	Date	Hour	Summary of Events and Information	Remarks and references to Appendices
			2/Lt. E. TURNER — M.C	
			2/Lt. E.R. ALFORD — M.C	
			No. 16895 Sgt. G. HUTCHINSON — D.C.M.	
			No. 4285 Sgt. W. PASQUILL — D.C.M.	
			No. 3215 L/Cpl. E. HUMPHRIES — D.C.M.	
			No. 29521 Pte. T. KILGALLON — D.C.M	
			No. 12762 Pte. C. SPEAKMAN — D.C.M.	
			No. 12650 Sgt. H. FEARNIOUGH — Bar to D.C.M.	
			No. 15126 Sgt. T. BARNES — M.M.	
			No. 15464 Sgt. J.A. TINSLEY — M.M.	
			No. 15790 Pte. F. CARTWRIGHT — M.M.	
			No. 17999 Pte. R. LEATHER — M.M.	

7th INFANTRY BDE.

25th DIVISION

8th BATTALION

LOYAL NORTH LANCASHIRE REGIMENT.

DECEMBER 1916

Army Form C. 2118

WAR DIARY
or
INTELLIGENCE SUMMARY
(Erase heading not required.)

Vol 15

8th (S) Bn LOYAL NORTH LANCS. REGT.

Instructions regarding War Diaries and Intelligence Summaries are contained in F.S. Regs, Part II. and the Staff Manual respectively. Title Pages will be prepared in manuscript.

Place	Date	Hour	Summary of Events and Information	Remarks and references to Appendices
In the Field	1/12/16		Relieved the 3rd Worcesters in Right Sub-Sector of LE TOUQUET line	
	2/12/16		Work on trenches - draining, revetting, and repairing.	
	3/12/16		Drainage getting much better. Salient still the worst part of trenches	
	4/12/16		Enemy badly damaged Salient by heavy firing of minenwerfer & aerial torpedoes (small - nicknamed "pineapples"). Rifle Grenades also thrown. Special working parties sent to help in clearing trenches and rebuilding. A small party turning out early next morning on land mine or portable charge with fuze and potato lights was found Mine, also a sandbag containing five hand grenades. Apparently they were disturbed by a patrol before they could do any damage. Casualties 1 killed and 9 wounded.	
	5/12/16		Batt. frontage shortened. Gave up left by frontage which was taken over. This was part of rearrangement of line due to a new Division (36th) coming into line on left of our Division. Our left boy. lodged in trench opposite bijou on a new frontage on LE TOUQUET - MOTOR CAR CORNER ROAD.	
	6/12/16		Usual work on trenches	

Army Form C. 2118

WAR DIARY
or
INTELLIGENCE SUMMARY

(Erase heading not required.)

Instructions regarding War Diaries and Intelligence Summaries are contained in F. S. Regs., Part II. and the Staff Manual respectively. Title Pages will be prepared in manuscript.

Place	Date	Hour	Summary of Events and Information	Remarks and references to Appendices
In the Field	7/12/16		Relieved by 3rd Worcesters. Went into billets at PONT DE NIEPPE.	
	7/12/16 to 12/12/16		All available men employed on sanitary work in town, R.E. dumps fatigues, drainage work on Bde. sector and work on communication trenches. Men get little rest.	
	13/12/16		Pioneers and small party of S.W.B. dirt cots in one of huts. We relieved 3rd Worcesters in front line trenches.) Enemy fire minnies at Salient. 2/Lt A.P. HILL wounded and 6 O. Ranks. Small wire cutting operation carried out against enemy trenches. Parapet breeched. Enemy replies by "minnies". Our wire damaged as in place. No casualties.	
	14/12/16			
	15/12/16 to 18/12/16		Usual work in trenches. Patrols fire enemy patrols active. Two drafts of "untrained" men received (93 first draft 16/12/16 40 second draft 18/12/16) Not available for front line trenches. Owing to outbreak of measles amongst 3rd Worcesters we were not relieved.	
	19/12/16		Wire cutting operations on enemy wire and demolition of parts of his front line operations due to Capt. C.T.S. MUNNIS starting firing halfan hour before our operations due to start. 6" Howitzers engaged minnies and did excellent work. So fine to house in FRELINGHEIN from which minnies fired badly damaged.	
	20/12/16		Very successful operation. Enemy probably regard as no retaliation	

Army Form C. 2118

WAR DIARY
or
INTELLIGENCE SUMMARY
(Erase heading not required.)

Place	Date	Hour	Summary of Events and Information	Remarks and references to Appendices
In the Field	21/12/16		Relieved by 3rd Worcesters. Battn. Support with two Coys in LE BIZET and two in Supporting Points now only held PATERNOSTER ROW, RESERVE FARM, and GUNNER'S FARM on left. Held the usual posts on right LYS FARM, STATION REDOUBT, and SEVEN TREES REDOUBT.	
"	25/12/16		In Bde Support during this period. two new dugouts opened up on the 23rd, and 6? on the 25th. Parties were sent to STN REDOUBT on three days for purposes of work.	
	26/12/16			
	27/12/16		Relieved the 3rd Worcesters. First Regt in the Trenches	
	31/12/16		Work in Trenches — draining, revetting and repairing. NAPOO AVENUE AND BARKENHAM AVENUE — Drainage getting much better. Salient of new part of the Trenches	

H.S. Evans 2/Lt &A/Adjt
8th Royal N. Lancs Regt

WAR DIARY or INTELLIGENCE SUMMARY

Army Form C. 2118.

8 L N Lanc Regt

Vol 16

Place	Date	Hour	Summary of Events and Information	Remarks and references to Appendices
In the Field	4/1/17		Battalion went into Brigade Reserve at Pont-de-Nieppe - Relieved by 2nd Worcesters Regt on the Right of ' officer and 8 OR received	New Year Hon. List ? see other Appendix
	5/1/17		Engaged on wiring parties on the trenches - Reinforcement of one officer received	
	6/1/17			
	7/1/17		Battalion went into the line,) Three companies in the first line and one in close support Reinforcement of one officer received Work of repairing trenches carried on, and mains opened up in the right sector, and in the left sector. In the SALIENT work of bridging craters carried by enemy heavy trench mortars was successfully carried out - Work in C gpo complete	
	12/1/17		Activity. Enemy guns were shelled in support trenches and part of WARPED AVENUE was damaged, and was repaired by working parties. Small shells 77mm were also shelled at STATION REDOUBT and SURREY FARM but with no material damage. Casualties. During the town of duty Casualties sustained 2 other ranks wounded.	
	13/1/17		Battalion relieved by 3rd Worcestershire Regt and came Battalion in Brigade Support -) Two companies in LE BIZET and two companies in the supporting Points - Reinforcements 3 officers and 66 other ranks received.	MJ

WAR DIARY or INTELLIGENCE SUMMARY

Army Form C. 2118.

Place	Date	Hour	Summary of Events and Information	Remarks and references to Appendices
	15/1/17		Battalion in Brigade Support. Work of repairing and making trenches carried on by D + D companies in the supporting line. Trenches 1 Officer and Lieut. Col. J.B. Rouat resumed command of Battalion on return from leave.	
	16/1/17			
	19/1/17		Battalion relieved by the 2nd (5) Batt. Loyal North Lancashire Regiment and the Brigade retired in the late for the purpose of training. Battalion proceeded to hutts at ROMARIN	
	17/1/17		Training carried out, the Battalion marching to training ground near BAILLEUL on alternate days for attack practice. The following drafts were received during the present: 1st Bn 10 O.R., 2nd Bn 68 O.R., 3rd Bn 63 O.R., Res. 6 O.R. — 1 Officer	
	23/1/17		Battalion engaged in sending up working parties to the line, and also in training the training area at BAILLEUL could not however be used.	
	29/1/17			
	31/1/17		List of Honours Gained during January. DCM 3847 C/R.S.M. J. Anderson " 16449 Sergt J. Walsh are Lewis Guns Battery	Mentioned in Dispatches Major A+J Erskine Major J.G. Wynne D.S.O Captain J. Ramsey D.S.O Captain A Spurgeon D.S.O.(2nd Tr.M. Battery) 14733 Q.C.S.M. J. Smalley 16451 Pte. E. Atherton J.B. Rouat Lt. Col. Comdg. 1st(S) Bn. Loyal Northern Reg.

AWARDS 423   BATTN. ORDER No. 82

Under authority granted by H.M. The King, the Corps Commander has awarded the Military Medal to the following N.C.O. and men :-

    27036 Sergt. BROSTER. A.

    15451 Pte. ATHERTON. A.

    23818 Pte. CHILTON. H.

    17620 Pte. STANLEY. F.

The Commanding Officer congratulates the recipients.

Army Form C. 2118.

1 LN Kenn Regt

WAR DIARY
or
INTELLIGENCE SUMMARY
(Erase heading not required.)

Instructions regarding War Diaries and Intelligence Summaries are contained in F. S. Regs., Part II. and the Staff Manual respectively. Title Pages will be prepared in manuscript.

Place	Date	Hour	Summary of Events and Information	Remarks and references to Appendices
ROMARIN	1 Feb 17		At ROMARIN CAMP conclusion of training.	
In the Field	2 Feb 17		Relieved the 13th Battn Cheshire Regt in the Ploegsteert Sector. Trenches in good condition though owing to intense frost little work was able to be done whilst a bright moon prevented patrols being sent out.	
	5 Feb 17		Battalion relieved in the line by 1st Wiltshire Regt and went into Brigade Support at CRESLOW FARM.	
	6 Feb 17		Wiring parties found by companies situated in the supporting Points	
	9 Feb 17		Relieved 1st Wiltshire Regt in the line. Two companies in the front line and two in support line, patrols sent out in front of the BIRDCAGE and wiring carried out. Wire cutting operations carried out by our French mortars and artillery.	
	10 Feb 17			
	13 Feb 17		Relieved in the line by 1st Wiltshire Regt & went into Brigade Reserve in REGINA CAMP working parties found for the line.	
	14 Feb 17			
	16 Feb 17		Raid carried out by the 1st Wiltshire Regt and 10th Cheshire Regt a party of the Battalion detailed to send up smoke cloud was not required owing to unfavourable wind.	
	17 Feb 17			
	18 Feb 17		Relieved 1st Wilts Regt in the trenches. A raid carried out on the right of the Battn by the 75th Bde caused Artillery retaliation. Casualties – 2 Officers – Lt HILL M.C. g/Capt SMITH (slightly at duty) and 13 other ranks.	

Army Form C. 2118.

WAR DIARY
or
INTELLIGENCE SUMMARY
(Erase heading not required.)

Instructions regarding War Diaries and Intelligence Summaries are contained in F. S. Regs., Part II. and the Staff Manual respectively. Title Pages will be prepared in manuscript.

Place	Date	Hour	Summary of Events and Information	Remarks and references to Appendices
In the field	19.6.17		Musical work on trenches, owing to thaw much work necessary. Patrolling and wiring carried out by night.	
	21.6.17			
	22.6.17		Relieved in the line by 3rd New Zealand (Rifle) Brigade. Battalion proceeded to ROMARIN CAMP.	
	23.6.17		Battalion moved back through BAILLEUL to the BERTHEN AREA	
	24.6.17		taking up billets in farms to carry out training.	
	25.6.17		Chimes & Parades.	
	26.6.17		Training programme carried out 9-1 daily with recreational programme in the afternoon.	
	28.6.17			

HONOURS

3215 S/C Hughes J.E Croix-de-Guerre.

J.B. Howard
Lt-Col. Comdg
8/451 Batt.
Loyal North Lancs Regt.

WAR DIARY
or
INTELLIGENCE SUMMARY
(Erase heading not required.)

Army Form C. 2118.

8 R* Lanc*s
Nov 18

Place	Date	Hour	Summary of Events and Information	Remarks and references to Appendices
BERTHEN	1st Mar.		Battalion in training. Route marches as a Battalion and with Brigade - Attack Practice in Training Area - Company training in Bayonet Exercises, Bombing, Musketry &c - Recreational programme carried out in the afternoon.	
LYNDE	11th Mar.		Batt* marched to LYNDE area to carry on training - Brigade Route March. Training continued in Bombing, Rifle grenade work under company commanders. Elementary outposts. Recreational programme in the afternoon.	
Sec Bois	18th & 19th Mar. 20th Mar.		Batt* moved to Sec Bois. B Company proceeded to Divl. Musketry School METEREN for training	
Outterssteene	21st Mar. 22nd Mar.		Batt* moved to Outterssteene Area. Batt* all at Baths - Training carried on.	
La Creche	23rd Mar. 30th Mar. 31st Mar.		Batt* moved to La Creche Area for training. Training carried on new billets & at training area BAILLEUL. Batt* inspected (24th) by Army Commander (2nd Army) General Sir HERBERT C*O* PLUMER B.C.B. K.C.B. A.D.C.	
KORTEPYP CAMP	31st Mar.		Proceeded to KORTEPYP CAMP to carry out work for II ANZAC CORPS.	
			AWARD DURING March.	Italian Decoration. Bronze Medal for Military Valour. 19628 Pte. R. Hutchinson

P. B. Hennessy
LIEUT COLONEL
COMMANDING 8th LOYAL NORTH LANCASHIRE REGT.

Army Form C. 2118.

WAR DIARY
INTELLIGENCE SUMMARY
(Erase heading not required.)

Instructions regarding War Diaries and Intelligence Summaries are contained in F. S. Regs., Part II. and the Staff Manual respectively. Title Pages will be prepared in manuscript.

[top right: 8/512 Royal Irish Regt — Vol 19]

Place	Date	Hour	Summary of Events and Information	Remarks and references to Appendices
NEUVE EGLISE.	1/4/17.		Sunday — Church Parade in the morning. — Working parties consisting of all the available men and the Battn. worked all night on digging an 8' deep cable trench at 6 point about 1000 yds J. of WULVERGHEM.	
"	2/4/17.			
"	3/4/17.			
"	4/4/17.		Night work on cable trench continued. — Companies also carried out Coy's. training during the day.	
LA CRECHE	5/4/17.		Battalion marched back to billets in the LA CRECHE area, near STEENWERCK.	
"	6/4/17.		Marched to billets at LE BIZET, "B" "C" + "D" Coys in billets, "A" Coy in supporting points behind the front line.	
LE BIZET.	7/4/17.		Training continued in the morning. Capt. T.M. FOOTE rejoined from Senior Officers course. — took over duties of 2nd in command from Capt. T. REES who resumed command of "C" Coy.	
"	8/4/17.		Church Parade for Coys in billets. — Reinforcement of 4 O.R. arrived.	
"	9/4/17.		Training continued. — 180 men sent to bathe at PONT de NIEPPE.	
FRONT LINE	10/4/17.		Relieved the 1st Wilts. in the front line between from the river LYS situated front LE GHEER. "C" Coy on the right, "D" night centre, "A" Coy left centre, "B" Coy on the left.	
"	11/4/17		Front line.	
"	12/4/17		Front line.	
"	13/4/17		Relieved at dusk by 10th Cheshire Regt., remained back to billets in LE BIZET. On Battalion in Bde. support. — "C" Coy took over garrison of supporting points with 2 sections in Hun REDOUBT, — 1 Platoon in RESERVE Farm, one platoon at LANCASHIRE SUPPORT; 2 sections at MAISON 1875. — Remaining platoon in LE BIZET. — "D" Coy. left 2 sections to garrison STATION REDOUBT.	

Army Form C. 2118.

WAR DIARY
~~INTELLIGENCE~~ SUMMARY
(Erase heading not required.)

Instructions regarding War Diaries and Intelligence Summaries are contained in F. S. Regs., Part II. and the Staff Manual respectively. Title Pages will be prepared in manuscript.

Place	Date	Hour	Summary of Events and Information	Remarks and references to Appendices
LE BIZET	14/5/17		Relieved from Bdes support at 12 noon by 3rd Wocester Regt. Marched back to billets at OUTTERSTEENE — bus cancelled during this town men to billets & 6 marched.	
St MARIE CAPPEL	15/5/17		Marched to billets at St MARIE CAPPEL.	
"	16/5/17		Weekly exam at 25th Division Musketry School.	
"	17/5/17		— Reinforcement of 4 O.R. arrived.	
"	18/5/17		Do.	
"	19/5/17		Do.	
"	20/5/17		Do.	
"	21/5/17		Do.	
"	22/5/17		Do.	
NOOTE BOOM	23/5/17		Marched to billets in the NOOTE BOOM area.	
"	24/5/17		Training resumed — 'A' 'B' Coys went to baths at OUTTERSTEENE. Capt O.H. HADLEY & Capt J.S. RAMSAY rejoined the Battn.	
"	25/5/17		Do. 'C' 'D'. Reinforcement of 14 O.R.	
"	26/5/17		Do.	
"	27/5/17		— Battalion marched to training area near BAILLEUL to carry out the attack practise from 9am to 1pm.	
"	28/5/17		Training in the morning — Attack practise in training area from 2.30pm to 5pm.	
"	29/5/17		Sunday — Church parade.	
"	30/5/17		Left NOOTE BOOM marched to billets in STRAZEELE area.	

J.B. [signature]
Lt. Col.
Commanding 8th (S) Bn. Royal Irish ~~Lanc~~ Regt.

Army Form C. 2118.

8 L N Lanc Regt

Vol 20

WAR DIARY or INTELLIGENCE SUMMARY
(Erase heading not required.)

Place	Date	Hour	Summary of Events and Information	Remarks and references to Appendices
STRAZEELE	1st/2nd April		Batt. in billets at STRAZEELE. Training carried out by companies in Bayonet Fighting, Rifle & Grenade work, Bombing, Musketry &c.	
LYNDE	3rd April		The Battalion moved to LYNDE on its way to the II Army Training Area	
TATINGHEM	5th May		The Battalion resumed its march and arrived at training area, being billeted in TATINGHEM.	
	6th May		Parade services in the morning. All arrangements made for 12 days Musketry training.	
			Programme of Army carried out, this included Musketry training. Batt. drill, visits of demonstration of attack at Down Berg school, talks given on the DUELMES RANGE, cleaning of attack practice. On one night march of companies on Cavalry Sch. was fired.	
	12th		Battalion practised attack on Bonjack Training Area.	
	13th		Arrived, namely RSM Probert & 25 other ranks.	
	14th		Training carried out by two companies, remaining two as work on filling in trenches at Bonjack Training area Bell on N.E. mines.	
	15th		Four bg. companies attack practice on Bell area in morning. Battalion moved into bivouac at night. 15th/16th completed practise attack as Batt. on 16th. Batt. party carried out later in the day.	
	16th			
LYNDE	17th 18th		Bonjack attack carried out in morning. Dismissal of Bonjack commenced. Batt. moved to LYNDE	

WAR DIARY or INTELLIGENCE SUMMARY

Army Form C. 2118.

Place	Date	Hour	Summary of Events and Information	Remarks and references to Appendices
STRAZEELE	19th		Battn. moved to STRAZEELE	
RAVELSBERG	20th		Battn. moved into Bivouac near NEUVE EGLISE - Capt R.J. CASH rejoined & took over duties of Adjutant.	
	20th to 24th		Battalion remained in Bivouac on RAVELSBERG road - about 2 miles W. of NEUVE EGLISE - working parties were provided for unloading ammunition about 400 men per day being used.	
NEUVE EGLISE	24th to 28th		The 7th Inf. Brigade relieved the 74th Inf. Brigade in the WULVERGHEM sector the 1st Wiltshire Regt. going into the trenches, 8th Loyal N. Lancs in Brigade Support at NEUVE EGLISE & the remaining 2 Battalions in Reserve at ALDERSHOT & BULFORD Camps. The battalion found about 500 men daily for work in forward area under 106 Coy R.E. On the nights of May 26 & 27 the village of NEUVE EGLISE was heavily shelled & the battalion (less H/Q) was moved into Bivouacs near the village.	
Trenches — WULVERGHEM Sector	28th		The battalion relieved the 1st Wiltshire R. in the trenches. relief was carried out successfully. 8 Officers & 92 O.R. were left at Transport Lines under Capt. O.H. Hindley to form a "B" Team. These proceeded on May 30 to MORBECQUE	

WAR DIARY

Place	Date	Hour	
Trenches – WULVERGHEM Sector.	28th		During the night of 28th the enemy bombarded our front trenches the damage done was however inconsiderable.
	29th		Day was quiet except for activity by an own artillery. At 10 pm the the battalion provided a covering party for R.E's who were taping out a new trench in front of original front line – work successful & completed by 2am
	30th		Day quiet. At 10 pm the battalion provided same covering party. The new trench was dug by about 1800 men of 7th Brigade. Work successful – completed by 2AM. At 3AM Enemy shelled our front line support line heavily with 5·9" shells until about 4.15 AM.
	31st		No unusual occurrence.

J.M Caldwell Major
Comdg 8/Royal N. Lanc R

3rd Worcrstershire Regiment.
1st Wiltshire Regiment
10th Cheshire Regiment.
8th Loyal North Lanc.Regt.
130th Field Company R.E.
106th Field Company R.E.

SC 992

7th Infantry Brigade.

The B.G.C. wishes to thank all ranks on the good work performed on the night of 30/31st., and to congratulate them on the siccess of the undertaking, thanks to the organization etc. made by the R.E. officers in conjunction with the excellent work performed by the troops and the silent and methodical execution of the plans.

Please communicate to all concerned.

May 31st 1917

(Signed) S.HAWKINS, Captain,
Staff Captain, 7th Infantry Brigade.

Copy to Brigade Major.

WAR DIARY or INTELLIGENCE SUMMARY.

Army Form C. 2118.

8 & 28 Lancs Regt
JUNE 1917

Place	Date	Hour	Summary of Events and Information	Remarks and references to Appendices
TRENCHES WULVERGHEM SECTOR	June 1		The battalion remained in trenches - Our artillery very active.) Nothing else to report	
	2		An enterprise was carried out in conjunction with the 3rd WORCESTER R. on the enemy trenches (NUTMEG TRENCH & NUTMEG RESERVE)	
			Object: to capture German prisoners & entr. German positions in NUTMEG TRENCH and NUTMEG RESERVE.	
			Party taking part in enterprise consisted of 100 men of D Coy under	
			Capt. S. RAMSAY D.S.O. & 2 Lt. WILLIAMS.	
			The enterprise by WORCESTER R. consisted of a smaller party. This enterprise was unsuccessful	
			by attempting to objective being on our Right.	
			The enterprise carried out by 8/L.N. LANCS did not succeed owing to	
			the party getting into our own barrage & having to return. Capt.	
			RAMSAY who was with the first wave being killed	
			2 Lt. WILLIAMS subsequently took out a strong patrol with the object	
			of entering German first line & retrieving the body of Capt.	
			RAMSAY but the Germans were by this time on the alert	
			& the party could not get in. 2 Lt. WILLIAMS was	
			killed on his way back to our lines	

Army Form C. 2118.

WAR DIARY
or
INTELLIGENCE SUMMARY.
(Erase heading not required.)

Place	Date	Hour	Summary of Events and Information	Remarks and references to Appendices
TRENCHES —	2		It is very much to be regretted that 2 very valuable officers were thus lost to the Battalion. Total casualties for this Operation were strangely not heavy.	
WULVERGHEM Section	3		At 6 AM the Battalion was relieved by the 2nd Battn. South Lancashire Regt & went to RAVELSBERG CAMP	
	3–6		Battalion at RAVELSBERG resting & refitting.	
	6		At 7.30 PM on 6th the Battalion moved up to the trenches to take part with the rest of the Division in the attack on the MESSINES RIDGE. The Battalion moved into assembly trenches (ONSLOW TR. & FUSILIER TR.) & assembly was complete by 12 MN.	
	7	3.10 AM	ZERO HOUR : Following the explosion of several of our mines & under cover of an intensive bombardment the attack was launched against the MESSINES RIDGE. Objectives allotted to this battalion together with 3rd WORCESTER REGT were the Enemy's 1st & 2nd lines (NUTMEG TR. & NUTMEG RES. TR.) These were captured with small loss by 2500 plus 7½ minutes & the whole Division then had strong & swept on capturing the Ridge & penetrating into the Enemy's position about 6000 yards	

Army Form C. 2118.

WAR DIARY
or
INTELLIGENCE SUMMARY.
(Erase heading not required.)

Place	Date	Hour	Summary of Events and Information	Remarks and references to Appendices
TRENCHES — WULVERGHEM Sector	7		The Battalion was now in position of Brigade Reserve to 7th Inf. Brigade, in front of Wulverghem: the 75th Inf. Brigade who had passed through captured the furthest objective.	
			The day of the 7th was spent in consolidating the newly won ground & the battalion was also called upon to supply carrying parties for the forward units	
	8		On the evening of the 8th orders were received to move forward at 9 pm & take over the line known as "the Black Line" from the 75th Inf. Bde. At 9 pm a heavy bombardment began & it was judged advisable temporarily to withdraw from movement. The bombardment slackened at 10 pm & the Battalion advanced. The battalion relieved the 8th L.N. Lancs & the 11th Cheshire R. Considerable difficulty was experienced in effecting the relief owing to lack of guides to bring in any reconnaissance & in consequence of mud: The relief however was reported complete at 3.15am & the hill & BLACK LINE	
	9		H/Q was first established in an open trench in the BLACK LINE	

WAR DIARY
or
INTELLIGENCE SUMMARY.
(Erase heading not required.)

Army Form C. 2118.

Place	Date	Hour	Summary of Events and Information	Remarks and references to Appendices
	9		Bat was subsequently moved to LUMM FARM. It had been intended to constitute a new Bork on the R near B "M Dryes" line for flank protection but on inspection this was found unnecessary as the New Zealanders on our right had already a trench which fulfilled all requirements. Fairly heavy & continuous shelling on & about the DOTTED line during the whole time it was held by the Battalion & we had many casualties occurred.	
	10		On the 10th inst the Battalion was warned for Relief - this was carried	
	11		Relieved by 8/ D. & W. Regiment on night 88 11/12. Total casualties for 48 hours tour in high & 6th inst. Killed Officers NIL O.R. 36. Wounded Capt. O.H. HADLEY - Lt. A.H. CHAWORTH-MUSTERS (Rgn. T.O) 2 Lt. E.V. EVERARD - 2 Lt. J.S. FLOOD - 2 Lt. T.A. GRANT Other Ranks : 98 Missing Officers NIL O.R. 7	

Army Form C. 2118.

WAR DIARY
or
INTELLIGENCE SUMMARY.
(Erase heading not required.)

Place	Date	Hour	Summary of Events and Information	Remarks and references to Appendices
WULVERGHEM	12		The Battalion was in Camp near NEUVE EGLISE WULVERGHEM	
NEUVE EGLISE	13		On morning of 13th, Batt. marched to Camp near NEUVE EGLISE where	
			it remained until evening of 14th	
Trenches	14		On the night of 14th inst. the Battalion relieved 2nd R.I. RIFLES	
	to		(74th Inf Bde) in the old German Trenches on MESSINES RIDGE	
	22		(OCTOBER REG. OCTOBER SUPPORT. REGINA TRENCH. OCTOBER TRENCH.)	
			The 7th Brigade was then in support to 75th Brigade & Battalion	
			were employed each night in working parties digging C.T's in	
			the forward area	
			There was considerable shelling in this area but few casualties occurred	
			On the night of 21/22 the Battalion was relieved by 36th Australian	
			Battalion & went in to Camp at RAVELSBERG	
RAVELSBERG	23/24		The Battalion marched to SWARTENBROUCK area on night 23/24	
	24/25		March continued on night of 24/25 to HAVERSKERQUE	
	25/26		" " " " LIGNY LEZ AIRES	
	26/27		" " " area LE WANEL - NOEUVEAUVILLE	
			GLEM - LILETTE	
			CAPELLE SUR LA LYS	

Army Form C. 2118.

WAR DIARY
or
INTELLIGENCE SUMMARY.

(Erase heading not required.)

Instructions regarding War Diaries and Intelligence Summaries are contained in F. S. Regs., Part II. and the Staff Manual respectively. Title pages will be prepared in manuscript.

Place	Date	Hour	Summary of Events and Information	Remarks and references to Appendices
CAPELLE SUR LA LYS Area	27 to 30		The battalion remained in the CAPELLE SUR LA LYS area for a period of training (duration probably about 2 weeks).	

J. B. Kennedy
LIEUT. COLONEL,
COMMANDING 8th LOYAL NORTH LANCASHIRE REGT

To all ranks of 25th Division.
───────────────────────

I can't let this day pass without writing a few words to all ranks and all Branches of the Service in the 25th Division.

The work done during the preparation for and during the actual assault to-day has been simply magnificent.

I cannot thank sufficiently the Divisional Staff, the Brigadiers and their Staffs, and the Heads and Subordinates of the other Branches and Departments. All arrangements were very carefully made and endless pains taken to make the enterprise the success it has proved. The Artillery and Trench Mortars have done grand work. The Engineers and Pioneers have worked wonderfully. The Signal Service has been absolutely tireless. The Supply and Ordnance Services have worked night and day for the comfort of the men. Last but not least the Infantry have been magnificent both during their preparatory work and during the assault to-day and I am proud indeed to be able to say that I belong to the Division.

To-day's work has been a very fine performance and it will have a more far-reaching effect than may at first be apparent. The people of Germany are getting into a very depressed state of mind, they are losing confidence in their Military Chief, and are beginning to be a bit doubtful about the ultimate success of their piratical "U" Boat campaign.

<u>German people began</u>

- 2 -

German people began to doubt the infalibility of its Army after its meeting with the British Army on the SOMME, and many excuses had to be made for its failure; ARRAS then came as a very serious eye opener and the Army itself began to lose confidence and when it became evident that we meant to attack the MESSINES Ridge, the German General Staff had to circulate information to the troops that a second ARRAS could never happen as certain new methods had been adopted which made the failure of the British Offensive absolutely certain.   To-day MESSINES and the Ridge have been taken in one hour forty minutes and it must now be even more apparent to both German soldiers and Civilians that the methods of their Military Leaders whether old or new fail to stop the British Army when it has set its mind on carrying out an enterprise and it is very possible that the blow you have helped to lay on this afternoon will go far towards bringing the war to a close by the end of this summer.

(Sgd.) E.G.T. BAINBRIDGE,
Major-General,
7/6/17.   Commanding, 25th Division.

8th Loyal N. Lancs Regt.

Army Form C. 2118.

WAR DIARY
or
INTELLIGENCE SUMMARY.
(Erase heading not required.)

JULY 1917   Vol 22

Place	Date	Hour	Summary of Events and Information	Remarks and references to Appendices
CAPELLE SUR LA LYS	1 to 6		The battalion remained at CAPELLE SUR LA LYS area carrying out training close order Drill - Elementary attack Practice - musketry. It was expected that the period of training would be a fortnight, orders were however received to move on 6th inst to take over part of line on IInd Corps front	
	6.		The battalion moved by motor bus to STEENBECQUE & was billeted at THIENNES	
	7.		moved continued by motor bus to POPERINGHE, thence by march route to DOMINION CAMP near BUSSBOOM.	
	Night of 9/10		The battalion together with 1st WILTSHIRE R. moved to YPRES taking over accommodation from 8th Division - 3/WORCS R & 10/CHESH. R. went in to the line in the HOOGE sector	
			During march up to YPRES very heavy shelling occurred - one shell fell very close to Battalion H/Q & badly killing Regt. Sergt. Major PROCTOR & causing 8 other casualties. Another shell fell almost immediately afterwards, killed MAJOR T.M. FOOTE who was moving forward along the road to get in touch with an company in front. Casualties were all evacuated fully though with an considerable difficulty	

Army Form C. 2118.

WAR DIARY
or
INTELLIGENCE SUMMARY.
(Erase heading not required.)

Instructions regarding War Diaries and Intelligence Summaries are contained in F. S. Regs., Part II. and the Staff Manual respectively. Title pages will be prepared in manuscript.

Place	Date	Hour	Summary of Events and Information	Remarks and references to Appendices
While at YPRES	10 to 14		The Battalion was required to find working parties in the forward area. The enemy shelling fire was very intense on back areas in YPRES, all roads & approaches & battery positions were heavily shelled suddenly. A number of casualties also occurred through gas shells, the new "mustard" gas being employed by the enemy.	
	14/15		On the night of 14/15 the Battalion relieved the 3rd Bn WORCESTER Regt in the Right Sub-Sector of the Brigade front.	
	18		A raid was carried out by 100 men of C Coy under 2nd Lt. BROWN and 2 Lt S. D. APPLEBY. Objectives: enemy's front & support line IGNORANCE TRENCH and SUPPORT. Object: to capture prisoners, secure identification, destroy kitchens. The Raid started at 10.30 pm (ZERO hour). All objectives were reached but enemy trenches found unoccupied. Dugouts were bombed. At ZERO + 5 minutes enemy put a heavy barrage on his own	

WAR DIARY
or
INTELLIGENCE SUMMARY.
(Erase heading not required.)

Army Form C. 2118.

Place	Date	Hour	Summary of Events and Information	Remarks and references to Appendices
	18		Front & support lines which caused our forty considerable casualties	
			Including 2 Lt S.D.APPLEBY wounded 2 Lt H BROWN	
			Other Ranks killed 2 wounded 19 missing 11.	
	19		In afternoon B & 19th 1 Coy was relieved by 3/WORCESTER R and	
			returned to YPRES	
	20		Remainder of Battalion relieved during May 19/20th returned to YPRES	
	22		The Battalion remained in YPRES until night 22/23 providing working parties in	
			forward area.	
	22/23		The Battalion returned to DOMINION CAMP near BUSSEBOOM	
	24th		The Battalion moved to Camp in RENINGHELST area	
	24-29		Resting & Refitting. No working parties	
	30		The Battalion & transport lines (horses) to area of BELGIAN CHATEAU near	
			YPRES, being the concentration area of the Brigade with a view to	
			active operations	

J.H. Caldwell Lt. Col.
Cmdg. 8 Loyal N Lanc R

WAR DIARY or INTELLIGENCE SUMMARY

Army Form C. 2118.

2nd (5) Bn Royal W. Lancs. Regt
AUGUST 1917

Vol 2

Place	Date	Hour	Summary of Events and Information	Remarks and references to Appendices
BELGIAN CHATEAU	July 31		3.50 AM on July 31 was the Zero hour fixed for the attack to be carried out by the Second & Fifth Armies East of YPRES. The 25th Division at Zero hour was in support to the 8th Division who were carrying out the attack on the enemy's front system. Were detailed to push on further should the 8th Division gain its furthest objective. At 7.50 AM the Battalion together with the whole Brigade Brunies moved up to HALFWAY HOUSE + remained there all day + during the night of 31/1.	
	Aug 1st		Orders were received to relieve the 2nd E. LAN. R. (8th Division) on the WESTHOEK RIDGE which had for some time gained by the 8th Division. Lt. Col. A.F.S. CALDWELL (in command of the Bn) was accidentally wounded on the night of July 31 & Major F.G. WYNNE took over command at 6.30 p.m. on 1st. The relief of 2nd E. LANCS. was successfully carried out but was very difficult owing to the lack of definite information about the position held by that Regiment & the fact that being was carried out in day light in full view of the enemy who shelled GLENCORSE WOOD. The Battalion remained in this position from 1st to 5th inst. The conditions were very bad owing to the weather & the difficulties of	

WAR DIARY or INTELLIGENCE SUMMARY

(Erase heading not required.)

Army Form C. 2118.

Place	Date	Hour	Summary of Events and Information	Remarks and references to Appendices
			getting up materials & supplies by all kinds. Our casualties during this tour were 3 Officers & 147 O.R. wounded to 7 Officers killed.	
			Officers wounded :- Lt. Col. A.F.S. CALDWELL (accidentally) 31.7.1917 Capt. C.P. TINDALL-ATKINSON 1.8.17 Lt. A. SUMNER 1.8.17 2 Lt. P.J. KNIGHT 1.8.17	2 Lt A.M. FAIRWEATHER 3.8.17 2 Lt R.V. GILLIATT 4.8.17 2 Lt H. HIELD 5.8.17
		5 h	On the night of 5th the Bath Bn. relieved the 2nd Royal Irish Rifles & returned to Transport Lines near BELGIAN CHATEAU where a hot meal was provided after which they continued march to WINNIPEG CAMP.	
		6 h to 9 h	The Battalion remained at WINNIPEG CAMP	
		9 h	On the evening of the 9th the Battalion moved forward to SWAN CHATEAU near YPRES relieving 2nd 5. LANCASHIRE R. They only remained here one night however & on the night of the 10/11th were relieved by the 2nd Bn RIFLE BRIGADE (8th division)	

Army Form C. 2118.

WAR DIARY
or
INTELLIGENCE SUMMARY
(Erase heading not required.)

Place	Date	Hour	Summary of Events and Information	Remarks and references to Appendices
STEENVOORDE	11		and went back by motor bus to STEENVOORDE. The Bn. 3 Battalion arrived B the Brigade remained in the forward area until the night of 12/13	
	12		Resting & refilling	
	13		Church Parade in the morning – no other parades. Training was begun. Time available for training not known but it is expected that it will be too short to permit of advanced work. Training Programme therefore on Drill – musketry; Physical Training. Bayonet fighting. Lectures.	
	19		Battalion marched at STEENVOORDE until 19th. inst. When they proceeded by march route to DEVONSHIRE CAMP S.E. of POPERINGHE	
	19-23		At DEVONSHIRE CAMP. Training carried out as at STEENVOORDE.	
	23		Orders were received to return to STEENVOORDE and Battalion returned to STEENVOORDE N.B the town to billets N. B the town	
	23-26		At STEEN VOORDE – Training carried out	
	27		Lt. Col. AFS CALDWELL rejoined the Battalion & took over command	RJc

Army Form C. 2118.

WAR DIARY
or
INTELLIGENCE SUMMARY
(Erase heading not required.)

Place	Date	Hour	Summary of Events and Information	Remarks and references to Appendices
	29		Orders received that the Brigade was to be placed at Disposal of 23rd Division - 8th L.N. Lancs & 1 Coy 15 Hants OTR the line in CLAPHAM JUNCTION area. Communications.	
	30		Borein advance failed & proceed up to the line.	
	31		The Battalion moved up to the line in trenches & relieved a Battalion of 23rd Division in front of GLENCORSE WOOD. Holding line.	

R) Cork Capt for Lt Col
COMMANDING 8th LOYAL NORTH LANCASHIRE REGT.

WAR DIARY
or
INTELLIGENCE SUMMARY

Army Form C. 2118.

8(S) Bn L.N. Lancs Regt

Place	Date	Hour	Summary of Events and Information	Remarks and references to Appendices
	15/9/17		Battalion holding the line in front of GLENCORSE WOOD. Battn organised into 3 companies to effect this. A coy was subdivided, and ½ coys posted to D y C respectively. B and C coys held the line, the right of B coy joining up with a coy of the 1st WILTSHIRE REGT, the left of C coy being in touch with the left (Ly) company of battels (ly night) with a Battalion of the 47th Division. D coy in reserve partly in the MENIN tunnel with Battn Headquarters, and partly in a trench close to Battn Headquarters. During the tour of duty the Battn on the right (on the left of this Battn) was relieved by a Battn of the 14th Brigade and the coy of the 1st WILTSHIRE Regt by the 2nd LEINSTER Regt (24th Division). Active patrolling was carried out during the hours of duty, a daylight reconnaissance by Capt R.T. REES giving valuable information regarding the advanced posts of the enemy in GLENCORSE WOOD. Enemy shelling confined to back areas, and district Tanks 300 yds from CLAPHAM JUNCTION. Enemy snipers active from INVERNESS COPSE during the first 3 days of the tour, believed to be concealed in a elevated oak Tank in front of our line, sniping ceased from this point during the last 3 days, enemy sniper either to his Battn being relieved, and the post exterminated. Our own artillery put up a practice smoke barrage on the afternoon of the 15th inst - Shelling carried out systematically by enemy	

Army Form C. 2118.

WAR DIARY
of
INTELLIGENCE SUMMARY
(Erase heading not required.)

Instructions regarding War Diaries and Intelligence Summaries are contained in F. S. Regs., Part II. and the Staff Manual respectively. Title Pages will be prepared in manuscript.

Place	Date	Hour	Summary of Events and Information	Remarks and references to Appendices
CHATEAU SEGARD	6th–7th		front and support lines, and on his back areas. There was great aerial activity on both sides, weather conditions being excellent. Casualties (Officers) 2/Lt. R.O. WEBER. Died of wounds. 2/Lt. P.M. TAYLOR WOUNDED. 2 officers sick. Other Ranks 6 killed 2 Died of wounds 14 wounded. During this period 13 O.R. arrived in a draft at the Transport.	
	8th		Battn. relieved by the 8th BORDER REGT during the afternoon and evening of the 5th, relief complete by 11.20 p.m. Battn. moved into bivouacs, and dug-outs at CHATEAU SEGARD.	
WIPPENHOEK	9th		Cleaning up & refitting. Battn. moved to CONNAUGHT CAMP, during the night the "B" team rejoined from MILLAIN in a draft of 3 (RSM Newton & 20 O.R.) joined from the Base. CHURCH PARADE and BATHS.	
CAESTRE	10th		Marched into camp at CAESTRE	
STEENBECQUE	11th		Marched into billets at STEENBECQUE	
BURBURE	12th		Battn. entrained 7th March arriving at BURBURE at 8.25 a.m.	
	13th		Training – Physical Drill, Bayonet fighting, Gunnery & Elementary attack practices.	
	15th		Church Parade	
	16th			
	17th		Gas Demonstration & Attack Practices – (Draft joined of 7 O.R.)	

Army Form C. 2118.

WAR DIARY
INTELLIGENCE SUMMARY
(Erase heading not required.)

Instructions regarding War Diaries and Intelligence Summaries are contained in F.S. Regs, Part II. and the Staff Manual respectively. Title Pages will be prepared in manuscript.

Place	Date	Hour	Summary of Events and Information	Remarks and references to Appendices
	18th / 20th		Training in Batt. area. Bombing - Rifle Grenades - Practice in the attack - Night Operations. Draft of 20 O.R. joined from Base.	
	21st		Bde Musketry competition at ALLOUAGNE. Rest of Batt. training in the attack.	
	22nd		Attack carried out on a ruined village on the LIERES-AUCHEL AU BOIS Road. (Draft of 5 O.R. joined from Base)	
	23rd		Church Parade. (33 O.R. joined from Base)	
	24th/25th		Training in Batt. Training Area.	
	26th		Divisional Fête at ALLOUAGNE at which the whole Batt. were present. Draft of 3 N.C.Os. joined from Base.	
	27th		Training in the training area. In the afternoon a scheme was carried out by the 7th Bde for testing extent of lateral & forward communications.	
	28th		An attack carried out on the ruined village as on the 22nd, at which the Army Commander was present.	
	29th		Training in Batt. area.	
	30th		Church Parade.	

A.J. Maxwell
a/Lt-Col.
COMMANDING 8th LOYAL NORTH LANCASHIRE R.

Army Form C. 2118.

WAR DIARY
INTELLIGENCE SUMMARY
(Erase heading not required.)

8th (S) Bn Loyal N Lancs Regt   Vol 25

Place	Date	Hour	Summary of Events and Information	Remarks and references to Appendices
BURBURE	1st Oct		Training carried out chiefly Battalion schemes in the attack. Ranges and Specialists under Specialist Offrs.	
	2nd Oct		Brigadier-General C.F. GRIFFIN DSO (the Brigade Commander) inspected Battalion & Transports. In the midst of the 3rd orders were received to prepare for an immediate move.	
BETHUNE	4th Oct		The Battn moved with the rest of the Bde to BETHUNE.	
	5th Oct		74th Inf. Bde. relieved the 6th Inf Bde (2nd Division) in the GIVENCHY-FESTUBERT sector. The Battn on arriving into Bde Reserve at GORRE relieving the 13th ESSEX REGT. Officers accommodated by the Left Subsector & making ground — Training carried on at GORRE.	
	10th Oct		Battalion moved up in relief of the 3rd Worcestershire Regt, in the in right of the Bde. 1st WILTS and Left were in the 4th PORTUGUESE BDE. Battn disposed as under:- A in the right. B in close support. C in the centre. D on the left.	
	11th Oct		Work in repairing, draining, revetting and wiring carried out. Patrols were pushed out each night and GERMAN patrols seen. One CANADIAN Mobile Artillery Sections — very quiet. Evacuations — 1 O.R. Wounded.	
	16th Oct		On the 17th the Battn was relieved in the line by the 3rd WORCESTERSHIRE REGT and moved into Bde Support. A. in 5 Redts ie HERTS REDOUBT – MARIE REDOUBT HILDERS REDOUBT – HUNT FARM GIVENCHY KEEP	

Army Form C. 2118

WAR DIARY
or
INTELLIGENCE SUMMARY
(Erase heading not required.)

Place	Date	Hour	Summary of Events and Information	Remarks and references to Appendices
	17th		B Coy. in old Brit: Front Line.	
			C } Coys. WINDY CORNER.	
			D }	
			Batt. Headquarters at WINDY CORNER.	
	22nd		Batts. outfit working & carrying parties for R.E. in strong enemy trenches.	
	23rd		Batt. relieved 3rd WORCESTERSHIRE REGT. in the line - on the right of the Batt.	
			1st WILTS and on the left were the PORTUGUESE BDE.	
			Batt. disposed as under:-	
			A on the right.	
			B in the centre.	
			C in close support.	
			D on the left.	
			Night in repairing, draining trenches, turning carried out. Patrols worked each night.	
			Hostile Artillery Snipers very quiet.	
			Casualties 4 other Ranks Killed.	
	29th		Battn. relieved by the 3rd WORCESTER REGT. and moving into Brigade Reserve at CORRE	
			Battn. find Prs at Chateau CORRE	
	31st		Battn. Engaged in Training chiefly Lewis Gun instruction, working & carrying parties for T.M. BATTERY.	

A.M. Marshall Lt.Col
3/4/17

Army Form C. 2118.

WAR DIARY
of
INTELLIGENCE SUMMARY
(Erase heading not required.)

8 L N Lanc Rg!
Vol 26

Instructions regarding War Diaries and Intelligence Summaries are contained in F.S. Regs., Part II. and the Staff Manual respectively. Title Pages will be prepared in manuscript.

Place	Date	Hour	Summary of Events and Information	Remarks and references to Appendices
GORRE	1st Nov		Training carried out chiefly Lewis Gun instruction musketry and carrying parties for T.M. BATTERY.	
	4 Nov		Batt moved up in relief of the 3rd Worcestershire Regt, on the night of the Batt 1st WILTS. and on the left were the PORTUGUESE BDE. Batts disposed as under:- A in close support B on the right C in the centre D on the left	
			Most mgsniping, observing, revetting, and wiring carried out. Patrols Retaliatory activity carried out along our front. T.M. Enemy trench mortars active - Batt relieved in the time by the 4th Staffs Regt who joined the Bde in place of the 3rd Worcestershire Regt who were transferred to the 74th Bde.	
	10 H		Batt in Bde Support - A & B Coys at WINDY CORNER. C Coy in O.B.L. D Coys in Keeps Battalion HQ at WINDY CORNER. The usual working parties were carried out for Tale & Tunnelling Coys R.E. Special forecast Bns ordered every to Consolidated European attack.	
	16 H		Batt relieved the 4th S. Staffs Regt. in the line. Coys disposed as under:- A - on the right B - in the centre C - on the left D - in close support	

Army Form C. 2118.

WAR DIARY
or
INTELLIGENCE SUMMARY
(Erase heading not required.)

Instructions regarding War Diaries and Intelligence Summaries are contained in F.S. Regs., Part II. and the Staff Manual respectively. Title Pages will be prepared in manuscript.

Place	Date	Hour	Summary of Events and Information	Remarks and references to Appendices
	16/h		Heavy French Mortars. Enemy any active damage By some to COVER TRENCH SHETLAND ROAD. BARNTON.	
			Artillery. Our 3". 4.5". 18 pounders fired in retaliation, and also carried out destructive fire on known targets and task areas.	
			Patrolling. Owing to the large amount of damage done to trenches and the work required, few were sent out, but for hostility - E-tony - covering parties were out every night - a reconnoitring patrol went out to an centre cops.	
			Casualties. 1 O.R. Killed. 4 " wounded.	
	22nd		Batt relieved by 9th S. Staffs Regt & went into Bde Reserve at GORRE, Transp carried out of Coys & working parties provided for R.E.	
	23rd		Major FAWCETT assumed command of Bn. Batt. vice Lt Col APS Gilmer (Lt Lancs)	
	27th		Batt. arrived at FOUQUEREUIL	
	28th		Batt. arrived at BUR BURE	
	29th		Batt. marched at REQLINGHEM.	
	30th		Cleaning up after march & reconnoitring of training areas & progressive training in the 1st Army Training Areas	

Signed ?ymme Major
Comdg 8th (S) Battn
The ?oyal N. Lancs Regt.

Army Form C. 2118.

Decbr 1917.

8th Bn. L.N. Lancs. Regt.

Vol 27

WAR DIARY
INTELLIGENCE SUMMARY
(Erase heading not required.)

Instructions regarding War Diaries and Intelligence Summaries are contained in F.S. Regs., Part II. and the Staff Manual respectively. Title Pages will be prepared in manuscript.

Place	Date	Hour	Summary of Events and Information	Remarks and references to Appendices
RECLINGHEM	1st.		Training. At 10.0 pm a warning order was received ordering the Bde to be in readiness to move by rail to the 3rd Army.	
PREDEFIN	2nd.		Battn. marched to PREDEFIN	
COURCELLES-LE-COMTE	3rd.		Battn entrained (less A coy) at WAVRANS, and travelled during the night & the 3/4th. at COURCELLES-LE-COMTE	
	4th.		Battn. detrained at MIRAUMONT and marched to huts at BARASTRE proceeding by march route.	
BARASTRE.	5th.		A coy joined the Battn. and the Bde moved into huts.	
	6th.		Battn. under orders for move. Officers & N.C.O's went forward to reconnoitre the LAGNICOURT SECTOR on the afternoon of the 8th inst.	
	7th.			
	8th.			
BARASTRE	9th.		Battn relieved the 1st NORTHUMBERLAND FUSILIERS (3rd Division) on night of the 9th. Dispositions as under:—	
			Rt Sub-Sector. 1st WILTSHIRE REGT.	
			Left " 8. N. LAN. Regt. (2 coys in front line, 2 coys in close support)	
			Bde Support. 4th. S. Staffs Regt	
			Bde Reserve. 10th CHESHIRE Regt. Bde H.Q. VAUX.	
			3rd Division.	
			On the left of the Battn. O.C. Rt Sub-Sector.	
			2 coys H.S. Staffs Regt at tactical disposal of " Left " "	
			2 " " " " " " " " "	
	10H.		Trenches in excellent condition, hostile artillery, T.Ms & Snipers quiet. In order to guard against a surprise attack, 4 posts were put out in front of Battn line.	
	11th.		Lt-Col. A.F.S. CALDWELL resumed command of Battn.	
	12H.		On the morning of the 12th the enemy attacked the Division on the left of the Battalion after an intense artillery & T.M. bombardment, he succeeded in capturing on sections of the front line & close support, and some prisoners remained in his hands.	

2449   Wt. W14957/M90 750,000 1/16 J.B.C. & A. Forms/C.2118/12.

Army Form C. 2118.

WAR DIARY
or
INTELLIGENCE SUMMARY

(Erase heading not required.)

Instructions regarding War Diaries and Intelligence Summaries are contained in F.S. Regs., Part II. and the Staff Manual respectively. Title Pages will be prepared in manuscript.

Place	Date	Hour	Summary of Events and Information	Remarks and references to Appendices
	13th		In order to extend the front of the Bde during this period two coys of the 10th CHESHIRE REGT were hurried into the section of trench on the left of the Battn, one coy being in the front line, and one in close support, these coys came under the command of the O.C. 8. N. LAN. R. — It was also decided to put out a belt of wire on front of the posts on the Battn front, and on the night of the 13th inst. a belt of wire was put out, this was completed on the night of the 14th inst making a belt of wire 1500 yds in length. The work was rendered very difficult owing to the extreme hardness on the surface of the 13/14 A.M.	
	15th		On the afternoon of the 15th inst a relief was carried out, and on completion the Bde was formed as follows:— Rt Subsector — 4th S. Staffs Regt. Lt " — 10th Cheshire Regt. Bde Support — 8. N LAN Regt. Reserve — 1st WILTS Regt. During the period in Bde Support 3 coys (A, C, D) were ordered to dig a new trench, this trench was completed on the morning of the 20/21st and was inspected by the G.O.C. Division on the morning of the 21st. Bn K 750 yds B coy was kept under the orders of O.C. 4th S. Staffs Regt during this period — On the night of the 21st the Bde was relieved by the 75th Inf Bde. The Battn was relieved by the 11th CHESHIRE Regt, and went into camp near FAVREUIL as Divl Reserve.	
FAVREUIL	22nd		Cleaning up + nothing.	
	23rd to 25th.		During this period in Divl Reserve, a fresh Bombing a route for Inward Cable was allotted to the Battn. Total Lnyth of Route 1850 yds 4ft 6in in depth.	

WAR DIARY

INTELLIGENCE SUMMARY

(Erase heading not required.)

Army Form C. 2118.

Place	Date	Hour	Summary of Events and Information	Remarks and references to Appendices
	26th		Christmas Day observed by the Battalion.	
	27th / 28th		Work on barrack huts continued and satisfactorily completed on the 29th of this 29H/30H.	
	30th		Sunday. No working parties.	
	31st		1 coy detailed for work.	

31st Dec. 1917

A. Mitchell, Lt Col
Comdg. 8th Battn.
The Loyal North Lancashire Regt.

WAR DIARY or INTELLIGENCE SUMMARY

Army Form C. 2118.

8 LN Lane Regt
1/1/28

Place	Date	Hour	Summary of Events and Information	Remarks and references to Appendices
FAVREUIL	2.1.18		Battn. pushed forward to reconnoitre lines prior to Battn. relieving the 13th Battn. in the LAGNICOURT SECTOR.	
	3.1.18		Battn. took over from 11th CHESHIRE REGT. Battn. disposed as follows: Rt Subsector — 1st WILTS Regt. Left " — 5th N. Lan. Regt. Battn. Support — 10th CHESHIRE Regt. Battn. Reserve — 4th S. Staffs Regt. Battn. engaged on strengthening existing wire. Patrols in front of Battn. front nightly. No contact with the enemy.	
	4.1.18		Battn. relieved by 10th CHESHIRE REGT. and became Battn. in Reserve at VAUX. 1 company occupied an tunnelled wood 6ft S.W.B. at 3rd H.Q. Remainder in doing defensive line. Battn. relieved by 11th CHESHIRE Regt. + moved into No. 5 Camp FAVREUIL. Whilst in Divisional Reserve engaged in trying + wiring the MORCHIES – VAUX line one day in three. When not engaged in working parties training carried out.	
	26th		Battn. relieved 11th Cheshire Regt. Battn. disposed as follows: Rt Subsector — 1st WILTS Regt Left — 5th N. Lan R. Battn. Support — 4th S. Staffs Regt Battn. Reserve — 10th Cheshire Regt. 30 yds Range Physical Training + Bayonet Fighting Squad + Platoon Drill. Company Drill.	

Army Form C. 2118.

WAR DIARY
or
INTELLIGENCE SUMMARY
(Erase heading not required.)

Instructions regarding War Diaries and Intelligence Summaries are contained in F.S. Regs., Part II. and the Staff Manual respectively. Title Pages will be prepared in manuscript.

Place	Date	Hour	Summary of Events and Information	Remarks and references to Appendices
	26th		Battn. engaged on clearing trenches which had fallen in as the result of heavy rain following thaw. On the night of the 29th a German patrol was observed by one of our forward posts. This party was fired on and one of the party was killed. The body was brought in & found to belong to 21st B.R.I.R. of the 16th BAVARIAN Division. (NORMAL)	
	31st.		The Honours List published during the month (New Year) included the following. Distinguished Service Order Lt-Col. A.F.S. CALDWELL. Military Cross Capt. & Adjt R.J. CASH. Capt. Rev. D. CONWAY (with 5th N. Lan R). Mentioned in Despatches Lt-Col. A.F.S. CALDWELL. Capt & Q.M. W.H.D. KING 13792 Sergt AIREY J. 10451 " SCHOFIELD.T.	

A.J. Marshall Lt-Col.
Cmdg. 8th (S) Battn. The Loyal North Lancs Regt.

WAR DIARY

INTELLIGENCE SUMMARY
(Erase heading not required.)

Place	Date	Hour	Summary of Events and Information	Remarks references to Appendices
	1.3.16		Battn relieved by 10th Cheshire Regt - moved into Bde Support	
	3.3.16		Orders being received for relieving the Batln. 1st Batln W. Rid Regt returned to VIII K Div Reserve & relieved by 1st Wilts Regt	
		9 am & 2.00 p	Battn dispatched to 7th Inf. Bde Nelson Rest	
			Battn moved to FAUQUEMBERGUES	
		3.00 p & 2.30	Drafts marched to 2/4th Br. 2/5th Battn. Light of horse remainder of Battn marched to BRUSSELS to take Group of MGC issued into MGC INTELLIGENCE BATTN.	
			[signature] Lieut. Colonel	Column from [?]
			[signature] D.S.O. PISCHWA 13	
			ABERDEEN	

1019 END

www.ingramcontent.com/pod-product-compliance
Lightning Source LLC
Chambersburg PA
CBHW081354160426
43192CB00013B/2404